A MIDSUMMER NIGHT'S DREAM

By WILLIAM SHAKESPEARE

Preface and Annotations by
HENRY N. HUDSON

Introduction by
CHARLES HAROLD HERFORD

A Midsummer Night's Dream
By William Shakespeare
Preface and Annotations by Henry N. Hudson
Introduction by Charles Harold Herford

Print ISBN 13: 978-1-4209-5258-2
eBook ISBN 13: 978-1-4209-5259-9

Cover Image: Titania and Bottom, from A Midsummer Night's Dream (oil on canvas), Fitzgerald, John Anster (1832-1906) / Private Collection / Photo © Christie's Images / Bridgeman Images.

Please visit *www.digireads.com*

CONTENTS

Preface

A MIDSUMMER NIGHT'S DREAM

Registered at the Stationers' October 8, 1600, and two quarto editions of it published in the course of that year. The play is not known to have been printed again till it reappeared in the folio of 1623, where the repetition of certain misprints shows it to have been printed from one of the quarto copies. Few of the Poet's dramas have reached us in a more satisfactory state as regards the text. The play is first heard of in the list given by Francis Meres in his *Palladis Tamia*, 1598. But it was no doubt written several years before that time; and I am not aware that any editor places the writing later than 1594. This brings it into the same period with *King John*, *King Richard the Second*, and the finished *Romeo and Juliet*; and the internal marks of style naturally sort it into the same company. Verplanck, however, thinks there are some passages which relish strongly of an earlier time; while, again, there are others that have such an energetic compactness of thought and imagery, mingled occasionally with the deeper tonings of "years that bring the philosophic mind," as to argue that they were wrought into the structure of the play not long before it came from the press. The part of the Athenian lovers certainly has a good deal that, viewed by itself, would scarce do credit even to such a boyhood as Shakespeare's must have been. On the other hand, there is a large philosophy in Theseus' discourse of "the lunatic, the lover, and the poet," a manly judgment in his reasons for preferring the "tedious brief scene of young Pyramus and his love Thisbe," and a bracing freshness in the short dialogue of the chase, all in the best style of the author's second period.

There is at least a rather curious coincidence, which used to be regarded as proving that the play was not written till after the Summer of 1594. I refer to Titania's description, in ii. 1, of the strange misbehaviour of the weather, which she ascribes to the fairy bickerings. For the other part of the coincidence, Strype in his *Annals* gives the following from a discourse by the Rev. Dr. King: "And see whether the Lord doth not threaten us much more, by sending such unseasonable weather and storms of rain among us; which if we will observe, and compare it with what is past, we may say that the course of Nature is very much inverted. Our years are turned upside down: our Summers are no Summers; our harvests are no harvests; our seed-times are no seed-times. For a great space of time scant any day hath been seen that it hath not rained." Dyce, indeed, scouts the supposal that Shakespeare had any allusion to this eccentric conduct of the elements in the Summer of 1594, pronouncing it "ridiculous"; but I do not quite see it so, albeit I am apt enough to believe that most of the play was written before that date.

The Poet has been commonly supposed to have taken the groundwork of this play from *The Knight's Tale* of Chaucer. But the play has hardly any notes of connection with the *Tale* except the mere names of Theseus, Hippolyta, and Philostrate, the latter of which is the name assumed by Arcite in the *Tale*. The *Life of Theseus*, in North's translation of Plutarch doubtless furnished something towards the parts of the hero and his "bouncing Amazon"; while Golding's translation of Ovid's story of Pyramus and Thisbe probably supplied hints towards the interlude. So much as relates to Bottom and his fellows evidently came fresh from Nature as she had passed under the Poet's eye. The linking of these clowns with the ancient tragic tale of Pyramus and Thisbe, so as to draw the latter within the region of modern farce, is not less original than droll. The names of Oberon, Titania, and Robin Goodfellow were made familiar by the surviving relics of Gothic and Druidical mythology. But it was for Shakespeare to let the fairies speak for themselves. So that there need be no scruple about receiving Hallam's statement of the matter: "*A Midsummer-Night's Dream* is, I believe, altogether original in one of the most beautiful conceptions that ever visited the mind of a poet,—the fairy machinery. A few before him had dealt in a vulgar and clumsy manner with popular superstitions; but the sportive, beneficent, invisible population of the air and earth, long since established in the creed of childhood, and of those simple as children, had never for a moment been blended with 'human mortals' among the personages of the drama."

HENRY N. HUDSON

Introduction

A Midsummer-night's Dream is first mentioned in 1598 by Francis Meres, in his *Palladis Tamia*. Two years later it appeared for the first time in print, in two nearly simultaneous quarto editions. Whether the second was issued by the publisher of the first—T. Fisher—or surreptitiously by some one else, only the printer, J. Roberts, being named, cannot be decided. It corrects several blunders, is in general far superior to the texts known to have been pirated, and was afterwards used as the basis of the first Folio. But it commits more blunders than it corrects, conventionalises without insight, and is on the whole decidedly the less authentic and original.

The play had already, as the title-pages of both editions attest, been 'sundry times publicly acted,' by Shakespeare's company. It continued throughout the greater part of the seventeenth century to be one of the most popular of his early comedies. The attraction lay chiefly in two features,—the fairies and the clowns,—and the subtle threads by which they are in woven did not prevent their being detached, adapted, and imitated for the benefit of the distinct audiences to which each feature specially appealed. Thus in 1602 the clowns' burlesque was imitated in the Oxford play of *Narcissus*; and after the suppression of the theatres furtive performances were ventured of a droll, afterwards (1661) printed as *The Merry Conceited Humours of Bottom the Weaver*. The fairy-scenes had a more illustrious after-history. Shakespeare's fairydom, composed, as we shall see, of many elements, took hold of the contemporary imagination, and has coloured all subsequent fairy literature. Even the splendid attempt of Spenser, a few years before, to found a new spiritualised Faerie in the minds of men, succumbed before the poetic realism of the *Midsummer-Night's Dream*, and Gloriana became an alien in the fairy world. The fairy poetry of Drayton (*Nymphidia*, 1627) and Jonson (*The Masque of Oberon the Fairy Prince*, 1611), of Herrick and Randolph, is of Shakespeare's school. Later, the play fell upon evil days and evil tongues. Pepys heralded the age of prose by pronouncing, in effect, upon the most poetic of plays Hippolyta's scornful verdict upon the clown's performance: 'This is the silliest stuff that e'er I heard' (*Diary*, 1662). As opera and operette (from 1692) it pleased the eighteenth century. With the dawn of the Romantic Revival the *Dream* found at length its fit audience. Wieland borrowed the elves in *Oberon* (1780); Goethe in the *Walpurgisnacht* of Faust ('*Oberon und Titania's Goldene Hochzeit*') fantastically sported with Shakespearean motives; Tieck adapted the play under the title *Sommernachtstraum*, and Mendelssohn provided worthy music, the overture in 1826, the songs in 1843.

Beyond the facts already mentioned, external evidence for the date of the play is wholly wanting, and the internal evidence is far from simple. Palpable marks of the young Shakespeare, as we have seen him in the three preceding comedies, everywhere abound: the symmetrical grouping, the interchange of a lyrical manner in the serious scenes with buffooneries in the comical ones, the tragic terrors rather gratuitously invoked at the outset and somewhat lightly dissipated at the close. The confusions of the Athenian lovers are a comedy of errors, actually produced by the fairy agency to which Antipholus of Syracuse in his despair attributed his own. Hermia, like Ægeon, stands under the threat of death. There is still little care for subtle study of character, and these Athenian lovers are not a whit more elaborated than those of Navarre and Verona. In spite of its two great creations, Bottom and Theseus, the *Dream* belongs clearly to an earlier phase than the first of the comedies of character, *The Merchant of Venice* (1596). But it stands hardly less apart from the three earlier comedies of intrigue in boldness of design and mastery of execution. Shakespeare's youth betrays itself perhaps in what he chooses to do or to leave undone, but not in his way of doing it. The verse may be rather lyric than dramatic, but it reaches heights of lyric loveliness, only paralleled in the probably contemporary *Romeo and Juliet*. On these grounds, the *Dream* may be safely placed within the limits 1593-95. More precise clues to the date have been sought in the various supposed allusions. (1) Titania's description (ii. 2.) of the bad weather provoked by the fairy brawls had a close parallel in the rains and floods of 1594; (2) Bottom's suggestion that the lion might frighten the ladies unless provided with a reassuring prologue, was perhaps an allusion to a similar scene at the baptism of Prince Henry at Edinburgh, in August 1594, when a triumphal car was to have been brought in by an actual lion, 'but because his presence might have brought some fear to the nearest,' his place was supplied by a Moor.

(3) Many features in the play suggest that it may have been composed for some marriage-celebration at Court. A wedding, announced with stately emphasis in the opening lines, is the focus upon which the whole action converges; and Puck's parting song has much of the air of an actual epithalamium. This hypothesis has naturally led to attempts to discover the actual marriage in question. Tieck proposed that of Southampton in 1598, Elze and Kurz that of Essex in 1590. Mr. Fleay more recently has argued for the marriage of William Stanley, Earl of Derby, 24th January 1595. The first two, besides being too early or too late, were secret marriages, and may therefore be left out of account. The third conjecture is more plausible both as regards the date and the occasion, Lord Derby's marriage having taken place at Court, and been, as Stowe says, 'most royally kept.' Shakespeare's company had, moreover, been the 'servants' of Stanley's elder brother till his death, some months before. Against these plausibilities must be set the facts that Shakespeare's company is stated to have played at Court on 5th January and 22nd February 1595, but not on 24th January, the date of the marriage;[1] and that the title-page of neither quarto contains any allusion to the Court performance, which on this hypothesis was the original occasion of the play.

A Midsummer-Night's Dream is, as a whole, one of the most original creations in the history of poetry; but its nucleus already existed in the noble opening of Chaucer's *Knightes Tale*, the home-coming and wedding of Theseus and Hippolyta, and several hints of the imaginings with which Shakespeare has embroidered this simple incident, are to be found in the sequel. None of Chaucer's Tales was more famous; it had twice been dramatised in Elizabeth's reign,[2] and

---

[1] Fleay, *Life of Shakespeare.*

[2] *Palæmon and Arcyte*, by Richard Edwards, 1566; *Palamon and Arcite*, acted at the Rose Theatre, September 1594. Both are lost. The second may possibly be subsequent to the *Dream* and a consequence of its success.

Shakespeare himself is thought to have shared in the fine Jacobean *Two Noble Kinsmen*. Plutarch's *Life of Theseus* (translated by North, 1579) was clearly known to him. Shakespeare's Theseus is neither the ruthless soldier of Chaucer nor the heroic Don Juan of Plutarch, but a spirit of the finest temper and the noblest breed who has played both these parts and put them definitely by. A single phrase reminds us of his deluded Ægles and Ariadnes; another, of the injuries he had done his future wife in winning her at the point of the sword. His union with Hippolyta marks his final emergence from the barbarisms and infidelities of his youth into mature humanity and loyal love. His relations with the Athenian lovers have tragic possibilities, like those of Chaucer's Theseus with Arcite and Palamon; but their peril lies no longer in the ferocity of Theseus, but in that of the law he unwillingly administers, and instead of being hardly won to qualified mercy by the tears of his wife and sister he himself 'overbears' the despotic vindictiveness of Egeus.

But Palamon and Arcite seem to have actually suggested the group of Athenian lovers in whose fortunes Theseus similarly intervenes on the eve of his marriage. Their rivalry in the love of Emilie reappears, heightened and complicated after Shakespeare's wont, in the double rivalry of Demetrius and Lysander for Hermia and Helena. Theseus' master of the Revels also bears the name chosen by Arcite in disguise.

The wedding festivities, as of no moment for the story, Chaucer had passed lightly by. Shakespeare availed himself of this opening for an unmatched comic interlude. Bottom and his crew are doubtless drawn from life, and with a still fresher and more native touch than the corresponding comic group in *Love's Labour's Lost*, whose absurdities still savour of the traditional braggart and pedant. And Bottom's 'translation,' which links him with the story of the lovers, is incomparably more dramatic, because it brings his character into vivid relief, than the blunder of Jaquenetta by which Armado involuntarily brings about the comic climax of the earlier play. The story of *Pyramus and Thisbe* has, moreover, as we shall see, a sly relevance to the solemnities which it relieves, hardly to be found in the corresponding mummery of the Nine Worthies. Shakespeare probably read it in Ovid (*Metamorphoses*, lib. iv.), but it was widely familiar both in Chaucer's *Legend of Good Women*, in Golding's translation of Ovid (1565), and in a ballad by Thompson, the two latter couched in a doggerel not greatly above the measure of Peter Quince.

For the country-bred Shakespeare, however, the wedding motive touched the springs of yet another world of poetry. Elves in Germanic folklore were wont to haunt weddings, and, on this hint, coloured perhaps by the myths of the classic Hymen, Shakespeare has made his fairies hallow the house with song and bless the bridal bed. To this the whole fairy action attaches itself. Shakespeare's fairydom is, with all its magical unity of effect, a very composite growth, and nearly all the fairy plot, as distinguished from the fairy ritual, is drawn from the alien worlds of Latin poetry or mediaeval romance. Shakespeare was here, however, only carrying a step farther a process of assimilation which had been going on for centuries. Even in Chaucer's day the Germanic elf-world was not intact; the name 'fairy,' drawn from the wholly unrelated 'fay,' or enchanter, of romance, was already synonymous with 'elf,' and the classical Pluto and Proserpina were the King and Queen of 'Faerie.'[3] Pluto, when Shakespeare wrote, had long been replaced by Oberon; but Oberon himself owed his translation from the homely German dwarf Albrich, to the feudal and courtly imagination of French romance.[4]

Shakespeare's Oberon is, however, still many degrees further than his namesake and probable prototype in *Huon of Bordeaux*[5] from the Albrich of German myth. Huon's Oberon is still a dwarf in stature and in temperament, capricious, ardent, and irascible, loading his favourite with magic gifts and kingdoms, and ordering his instant execution for a supposed slight. Shakespeare's Oberon has the caprice without the violence; he displays mild beneficence towards the lovers, and calculated malice towards his queen. It seems as if Shakespeare had already devised a fairy psychology, and meant their attenuated emotions to emphasise their diminutive forms.

On the other hand, he adopted to the full the Romance scheme of a fairy-court, and brilliantly extended it by turning the rustic Puck, familiar to every English homestead, into Oberon's court-jester. 'I jest for Oberon and make him smile,' is Robin's description of his quality. Yet he remains for the most part little removed from his folk-lore prototype. It is only in the epilogue that he becomes, at parting, a mouthpiece for the quintessence of fairy-poetry.

Shakespeare's elf-queen seems to be more original than either. Tradition had less definitely fixed her character. Spenser had quite recently (1590) been able to apply the name to a being as little related to the legendary mistress of Thomas of Ercildoun as to Chaucer's Proserpina. Shakespeare himself gave her a Puck character as Mab in *Romeo and Juliet*. Classical scholars widely connected her with Diana.

---

[3] *Marchantes Tale, CT.*, E. 2227.

[4] This romance was translated by Lord Berners about 1540, and, in this form, repeatedly reprinted in Shakespeare's time, The third edition (the earliest extant) appeared in 1601. This was doubtless his immediate sources for Oberon. Greene had introduced Oberon as a chorus into his *James IV.*; and another recent play (now lost) had dealt with the King of the Fairies.

[5] Albrich's name implies that he must have originally been regarded as an 'elf-king'; but all trace of that dignity seems to have vanished in the German popular epic. Many other elf kings were known to Germanic mythology.

Titania is distinct from all these, but she seems to have affinities both with Diana and Proserpina. Like the queen of Hades, Shakespeare's fairies are of the night; they 'run from the presence of the sun, following darkness like a dream.' It was an easy step thence to bring them into a special relation to the moon, and thus they are made to pursue the chariot of the 'triple Hecate,' to sing hymns and carols to her, or neglect to sing them (ii. 1.). The poet of the *Midsummer-Night's Dream* was evidently attracted by the classical legends of the Moon, and Lyly's mythic drama on the Endymion story had probably contributed to the attraction. This aspect of his fairydom seems to have had its share in suggesting the name Titania, which he found in Ovid's *Metamorphoses* (iii. 173) as a synonym for Diana. Titania herself is, however, a very different being from the chaste maiden-deity. She is no goddess but a fairy, childlike in her innocence and her impulsiveness and, above all, helplessly subdued by the shafts of that casual and irrational love which the 'cold beams of the watery moon' had instantly quenched. But if she is not 'cold' she is the embodiment of feminine daintiness and delicacy; and all about her is imagined with an exquisite instinct for the elemental life of flower and insect and all the dainty and delicate things of nature.[6]

One flower, however, which plays a notable part in the plot, carries us back to myth.

The *love-juice* with which Puck anointed the eyes of the lovers and Titania was first brought into connection with fairy-lore by Shakespeare. It was perhaps suggested by a passage in the *Diana* of Montemayor (tr. 1579), a book which the *Two Gentlemen* shows him to have known. Upon this juice and its effects the whole plot turns. The attempts of Warburton and Halpin to read complex personal allusions into the pretty myth of the little western flower beyond the obvious compliment to Elizabeth, are therefore open to grave doubt. With the same delight in blending classical and romantic myths which marks his handling of the fairy world, Shakespeare sought a link between the classical and the romance symbols for the caprice and incalculableness of love,—between the arrow of Cupid and the love-juice. Such a link he found in the country name for the pansy—'love in idleness.' It receives the arrow and yields the juice. Cupid himself, the boy, is replaced by the king of the childlike fairies, and in Oberon's hands the juice provokes sudden accesses of unreasoning love. From these wayward caprices of passion, Theseus and Hippolyta, once sufficiently subject to them, now stand severely apart. They can afford to look down upon the delusive 'imagination' of the lover who sees Helen in a

---

[6] The last clause is borrowed from Mr. E. K. Chambers' admirable edition of this play (Blackie), to which this Introduction, and the above paragraph in particular, owes several suggestions.

brow of Egypt, or an 'angel' in an ass. And both the clear-eyed lovers and those whom imagination deludes are admirably set off by the 'crew of patches' who are deluded by the want of it. They see nothing but a brow of Egypt in Helen; their leader calls for provender in the very arms of the fairy-queen; the enactor of the lion explains that he is Snug the joiner; and the play itself is a travesty of love so palpably gross that, instead of captivating the imagination, it requires the active exercise of imagination to lend it the semblance of life.

Thus that interweaving of lyric love-scenes with clownish humours, in which the Elizabethans delighted, gradually became in Shakespeare's hands no mere relieving contrast of grave and gay, but a subtle instrument of poetic speech; and in none of the early comedies was it used with art so fine as in the present play, where the elements appear at first to be mixed with the fantastic incoherence befitting its name.

CHARLES HAROLD HERFORD

1901.

A MIDSUMMER NIGHT'S DREAM

DRAMATIS PERSONAE.

THESEUS, *Duke of Athens.*
EGEUS, *Father to Hermia.*
LYSANDER, *in love with Hermia.*
DEMETRIUS, *in love with Hermia.*
PHILOSTRATE, *Master of the Revels to Theseus.*
QUINCE, *the Carpenter.*
SNUG, *the Joiner.*
BOTTOM, *the Weaver.*
FLUTE, *the Bellows-mender.*
SNOUT, *the Tinker.*
STARVELING, *the Tailor.*

HIPPOLYTA, *Queen of the Amazons.*
HERMIA, *in love with Lysander.*
HELENA, *in love with Demetrius.*

OBERON, *King of the Fairies.*
TITANIA, *Queen of the Fairies.*
PUCK, *or* ROBIN GOODFELLOW, *a Fairy.*
PEAS-BLOSSOM, *Fairy.*
COBWEB, *Fairy.*
MOTH, *Fairy.*
MUSTARDSEED, *Fairy.*

PYRAMUS, THISBE, WALL, MOONSHINE, LION, *Characters in the Interlude performed by the Clowns.*

Other Fairies attending their King and Queen. Attendants on Theseus and Hippolyta.

SCENE: *Athens, and a Wood near it.*

ACT I.

SCENE I.

Athens. A Room in the Palace of THESEUS.

[*Enter* THESEUS, HIPPOLYTA, PHILOSTRATE, *and*
ATTENDANTS.]

THESEUS. Now, fair Hippolyta, our nuptial hour
Draws on apace; four happy days bring in
Another moon; but, oh, methinks, how slow
This old moon wanes! she lingers my desires,
Like to a step-dame or a dowager,[1]
Long withering out a young man's revenue.
HIPPOLYTA. Four days will quickly steep themselves in nights;
Four nights will quickly dream away the time;
And then the moon, like to a silver bow
New bent in heaven, shall behold the night
Of our solemnities.
THESEUS. Go, Philostrate,
Stir up the Athenian youth to merriments;
Awake the pert[2] and nimble spirit of mirth;
Turn melancholy forth to funerals—
The pale companion is not for our pomp.—[*Exit* PHILOSTRATE.]
Hippolyta, I woo'd thee with my sword,
And won thy love doing thee injuries;
But I will wed thee in another key,
With pomp, with triumph,[3] and with revelling.

[*Enter* EGEUS, HERMIA, LYSANDER, *and* DEMETRIUS.]

EGEUS. Happy be Theseus, our renowned Duke![4]

---

[1] A *dowager* is a widow with rights of dower, that is, with a portion of her husband's property secured to her by law. Of course, so long as she lives, a part of the inheritance is withheld from the children, whose revenue is said to be *withered out*, because their youth gets withered while they are waiting for it.
[2] *Pert* had not always the ill meaning now attached to it. Skinner derives it from the Latin *peritus*, which means *expert, skilful, prompt.*
[3] *Triumph* was used in a much more inclusive sense than it now bears; for various kinds of festive or public *display ox pageantry.*
[4] The application of *duke* to the heroes of antiquity was quite common; the word being from the Latin *dux*, which means a chief or leader of any sort. Thus in I *Chronicles*, i. 51, we have a list of "the *dukes* of Edom."

THESEUS. Thanks, good Egeus: what's the news with thee?
EGEUS. Full of vexation come I, with complaint
  Against my child, my daughter Hermia.—
  Stand forth, Demetrius.—My noble lord,
  This man hath my consent to marry her:—
  Stand forth, Lysander;—and, my gracious duke,
  This man hath bewitch'd the bosom of my child.
  Thou, thou, Lysander, thou hast given her rhymes,
  And interchang'd love-tokens with my child:
  Thou hast by moonlight at her window sung,
  With feigning voice, verses of feigning love;[5]
  And stol'n the impression of her fantasy
  With bracelets of thy hair, rings, gauds, conceits,
  Knacks, trifles, nosegays, sweetmeats,—messengers
  Of strong prevailment in unharden'd youth;—
  With cunning hast thou filch'd my daughter's heart;
  Turned her obedience, which is due to me,
  To stubborn harshness.—And, my gracious duke,
  Be it so she will not here before your grace
  Consent to marry with Demetrius,
  I beg the ancient privilege of Athens,—
  As she is mine I may dispose of her:
  Which shall be either to this gentleman
  Or to her death; according to our law
  Immediately provided in that case.
THESEUS. What say you, Hermia? be advised,[6] fair maid:
  To you your father should be as a god;
  One that compos'd your beauties: yea, and one
  To whom you are but as a form in wax,
  By him imprinted, and within his power
  To leave the figure, or disfigure it.[7]
  Demetrius is a worthy gentleman.
HERMIA. So is Lysander.
THESEUS. In himself he is:
  But, in this kind, wanting your father's voice,
  The other must be held the worthier.

---

[5] According to present usage, this should be "verses of *feigned* love." Probably it is but an instance of the indifferent use of the active and passive forms so common in the Poet's time. So we have *discontenting* for *discontented*, and *all-obeying* for *all-obeyed*.

[6] *Be advised* is old language for *bethink yourself*, that is, *deliberate* or *consider*. Very often so in Shakespeare.

[7] The language is something odd and obscure; but the meaning appears to be, "It is in his power either to let the form remain as is, that is, to leave it undefaced, or to destroy it altogether." In the Poet's earlier period, such jingles as *figure* and *disfigure* were too much affected by him.

HERMIA. I would my father look'd but with my eyes.
THESEUS. Rather your eyes must with his judgment look.
HERMIA. I do entreat your grace to pardon me.
  I know not by what power I am made bold,
  Nor how it may concern my modesty
  In such a presence here to plead my thoughts:
  But I beseech your grace that I may know
  The worst that may befall me in this case
  If I refuse to wed Demetrius.
THESEUS. Either to die the death, or to abjure
  For ever the society of men.
  Therefore, fair Hermia, question your desires,
  Know of your youth, examine well your blood,[8]
  Whether, if you yield not to your father's choice,
  You can endure the livery of a nun;
  For aye to be shady cloister mew'd,[9]
  To live a barren sister all your life,
  Chanting faint hymns to the cold, fruitless moon.
  Thrice-blessed they that master so their blood,
  To undergo such maiden pilgrimage:
  But earthlier-happy[10] is the rose distill'd
  Than that which, withering on the virgin thorn,
  Grows, lives, and dies, in single blessedness.
HERMIA. So will I grow, so live, so die, my lord,
  Ere I will yield my virgin patent up
  Unto his lordship, whose unwished yoke
  My soul consents not to give sovereignty.[11]
THESEUS. Take time to pause; and by the next new moon,—
  The sealing-day betwixt my love and me
  For everlasting bond of fellowship,—
  Upon that day either prepare to die
  For disobedience to your father's will;
  Or else to wed Demetrius, as he would;
  Or on Diana's altar to protest
  For aye austerity and single life.
DEMETRIUS. Relent, sweet Hermia;—and, Lysander, yield
  Thy crazed title to my certain right.
LYSANDER. You have her father's love, Demetrius;

---

[8] *Blood* was continually put for *passions*, *impulses*, and *affections*.
[9] To *mew* was a term in falconry; a *mew* being a *cage* or *coop* in which hawks were confined during the season of moulting.
[10] The meaning probably is, "happy in a more earthly and perishable kind of happiness."
[11] *Lordship* here means *dominion* or *government*; and *give* is used with two accusatives, *yoke* and *sovereignty*.

Let me have Hermia's: do you marry him.
EGEUS. Scornful Lysander! true, he hath my love;
    And what is mine my love shall render him;
    And she is mine; and all my right of her
    I do estate unto Demetrius.
LYSANDER. I am, my lord, as well deriv'd as he,
    As well possess'd; my love is more than his;
    My fortunes every way as fairly rank'd,
    If not with vantage, as Demetrius's;
    And, which is more than all these boasts can be,
    I am belov'd of beauteous Hermia:
    Why should not I then prosecute my right?
    Demetrius, I'll avouch it to his head,
    Made love to Nedar's daughter, Helena,
    And won her soul; and she, sweet lady, dotes,
    Devoutly dotes, dotes in idolatry,
    Upon this spotted[12] and inconstant man.
THESEUS. I must confess that I have heard so much,
    And with Demetrius thought to have spoke thereof;
    But, being over-full of self-affairs,
    My mind did lose it.—But, Demetrius, come;
    And come, Egeus; you shall go with me;
    I have some private schooling for you both.—
    For you, fair Hermia, look you arm yourself
    To fit your fancies to your father's will,
    Or else the law of Athens yields you up,—
    Which by no means we may extenuate,—
    To death, or to a vow of single life.—
    Come, my Hippolyta: what cheer, my love?
    Demetrius, and Egeus, go along;
    I must employ you in some business[13]
    Against our nuptial, and confer with you
    Of something nearly that concerns yourselves.
EGEUS. With duty and desire we follow you.

    [*Exeunt* THESEUS, HIPPOLYTA, EGEUS, DEMETRIUS, *and*
        Train.]

LYSANDER. How now, my love! why is your cheek so pale?
    How chance the roses there do fade so fast?
HERMIA. Belike for want of rain, which I could well

---

[12] *Spotted* for *wicked* or *false*, the opposite of *spotless*. So in Cavendish's *Metrical Visions*: "*Spotted* with pride, viciousness, and cruelty."
[13] Here, as in many other places, *business* is a trisyllable.

Beteem[14] them from the tempest of my eyes.
LYSANDER. Ah me! for aught that I could ever read,
Could ever hear by tale or history,
The course of true love never did run smooth:
But either it was different in blood,—
HERMIA. O cross! Too high to be enthrall'd to low!
LYSANDER. Or else misgraffed in respect of years;—
HERMIA. O spite! Too old to be engag'd to young!
LYSANDER. Or else it stood upon the choice of friends:
HERMIA. O hell! to choose love by another's eye!
LYSANDER. Or, if there were a sympathy in choice,
War, death, or sickness, did lay siege to it,
Making it momentary[15] as a sound,
Swift as a shadow, short as any dream;
Brief as the lightning in the collied[16] night
That, in a spleen,[17] unfolds both heaven and earth,
And ere a man hath power to say, *Behold!*
The jaws of darkness do devour it up:
So quick bright things come to confusion.
HERMIA. If then true lovers have ever cross'd,
It stands as an edict in destiny:
Then let us teach our trial patience,[18]
Because it is a customary cross;
As due to love as thoughts, and dreams, and sighs,
Wishes and tears, poor fancy's[19] followers.
LYSANDER. A good persuasion; therefore, hear me, Hermia.

---

[14] *Beteem* here clearly has the sense of *allow* or *permit*; as in *Hamlet*, i. 2: "So loving to my mother, that he might not *beteem* the winds of heaven visit her face too roughly."

[15] *Momentany* is an old form of *momentary*.

[16] *Smutted* or *black*; a word derived from the collieries.

[17] *Spleen* for *a fit of passion* or *violence*, because the spleen was supposed to be the special seat of eruptive or explosive emotions. So in *King John*, ii. 1:

> This union shall do more than battery can
> To our fast-closed gates; for, at this match,
> With swifter *spleen* than powder can enforce,
> The mouth of passage shall we fling wide ope,
> And give you entrance.

[18] The old poets very often make two syllables where modern usage allows but one. So, here, *patience* is properly a trisyllable. Various other words ending in *-ience* are sometimes used thus by Shakespeare; as also many words ending in *-ion*, *-ian*, and *-ious*. So it is with *confusion*, third line above.

[19] The Poet often uses *fancy* for *love*. So, afterwards, in this play: "Fair Helena in *fancy* following me." And in the celebrated passage applied to Queen Elizabeth: "In maiden meditation *fancy*-free."

I have a widow aunt, a dowager
Of great revenue,[20] and she hath no child:
From Athens is her house remote seven leagues;
And she respects[21] me as her only son.
There, gentle Hermia, may I marry thee;
And to that place the sharp Athenian law
Cannot pursue us. If thou lovest me then,
Steal forth thy father's house tomorrow night;
And in the wood, a league without the town,
Where I did meet thee once with Helena,
To do observance to a morn of May,[22]
There will I stay for thee.
HERMIA. My good Lysander!
I swear to thee by Cupid's strongest bow,
By his best arrow, with the golden head,
By the simplicity of Venus' doves,
By that which knitteth souls and prospers loves,
And by that fire which burn'd the Carthage queen,
When the false Trojan under sail was seen,—
By all the vows that ever men have broke,
In number more than ever women spoke,—
In that same place thou hast appointed me,
Tomorrow truly will I meet with thee.
LYSANDER. Keep promise, love. Look, here comes Helena.

---

[20] This word has occurred once before, but with the accent on the first syllable: here the accent is on the second syllable, as it ought to be. Shakespeare has it repeatedly in both ways: all the other English poets, I think, used it as in this place; at least so I have marked it in Spenser, Daniel, Dryden, Young, and Thomson. I have not met with the word in Milton's poetry, or in Wordsworth's.

[21] To *respect* in the sense of to *regard*; the two words being formerly used as equivalent expressions.

[22] This refers to the old English custom of observing May-day, as it was called, with a frolic in the fields and woods. Stowe, the chronicler, tells us how our ancestors were wont to go out into "the sweet meadows and green woods, there to rejoice their spirits with the beauty and savour of sweet flowers, and with the harmony of birds praising God in their kind." The celebration of May-day in this manner was a favourite theme with the old poets from Chaucer downwards. Wordsworth sings it charmingly in his two *Odes to May*; one stanza of which I must add:

> Time was, blest Power? when youths and maids
>   At peep of dawn would rise
> And wander forth, in forest glades
>   Thy birth to solemnize.
> Though mute the song,—to grace the rite
>   Untouch'd the hawthorn bough,
> Thy Spirit triumphs o'er the slight;
>   Man changes, but not thou.

[*Enter* HELENA.]

HERMIA. God speed fair Helena! Whither away?
HELENA. Call you me fair? that fair again unsay.
Demetrius loves your fair. O happy fair![23]
Your eyes are lode-stars;[24] and your tongue's sweet air
More tuneable than lark to shepherd's ear,
When wheat is green, when hawthorn buds appear.
Sickness is catching: O, were favour[25] so,
Yours would I catch, fair Hermia, ere I go;
My ear should catch your voice, my eye your eye,
My tongue should catch your tongue's sweet melody.
Were the world mine, Demetrius being bated,
The rest I'd give to be to you translated.
O, teach me how you look; and with what art
You sway the motion of Demetrius' heart!
HERMIA. I frown upon him, yet he loves me still.
HELENA. O that your frowns would teach my smiles such skill!
HERMIA. I give him curses, yet he gives me love.
HELENA. O that my prayers could such affection move!
HERMIA. The more I hate, the more he follows me.
HELENA. The more I love, the more he hateth me.
HERMIA. His folly, Helena, is no fault of mine.
HELENA. None, but your beauty: would that fault were mine!
HERMIA. Take comfort; he no more shall see my face;
Lysander and myself will fly this place.—
Before the time I did Lysander see,
Seem'd Athens as a paradise to me:
O, then, what graces in my love do dwell,
That he hath turn'd a heaven unto hell!
LYSANDER. Helen, to you our minds we will unfold:
To-morrow night, when Phoebe doth behold
Her silver visage in the watery glass,
Decking with liquid pearl the bladed grass,—
A time that lovers' flights doth still conceal,—
Through Athens' gates have we devis'd to steal.
HERMIA. And in the wood where often you and I
Upon faint primrose beds were wont to lie,
Emptying our bosoms of their counsel sweet,

---

[23] *Fair* for *fairness* or *beauty*; a common usage of the time.
[24] The *lode-star* is the *leading* or *guiding* star; that is, the *polar star*. The magnet is for the same reason called the *lode*-stone.
[25] *Favour* here has reference to the general aspect, and means about the same as *looks* or *personal appearance*. Repeatedly so.

There my Lysander and myself shall meet:
And thence from Athens turn away our eyes,
To seek new friends and stranger companies.²⁶
Farewell, sweet playfellow: pray thou for us,
And good luck grant thee thy Demetrius!—
Keep word, Lysander: we must starve our sight
From lovers' food, till morrow deep midnight.
LYSANDER. I will, my Hermia.—[*Exit* HERMIA.]
      Helena, adieu:
As you on him, Demetrius dote on you! [*Exit.*]
HELENA. How happy some o'er other some can be!
Through Athens I am thought as fair as she.
But what of that? Demetrius thinks not so;
He will not know what all but he do know.
And as he errs, doting on Hermia's eyes,
So I, admiring of his qualities.
Things base and vile, holding no quantity,²⁷
Love can transpose to form and dignity.
Love looks not with the eyes, but with the mind;
And therefore is wing'd Cupid painted blind.
Nor hath love's mind of any judgment taste;
Wings and no eyes figure unheedy haste:
And therefore is love said to be a child,
Because in choice he is so oft beguil'd.
As waggish boys in game themselves forswear,
So the boy Love is perjur'd everywhere:
For ere Demetrius look'd on Hermia's eyne,²⁸
He hail'd down oaths that he was only mine;
And when this hail some heat from Hermia felt,
So he dissolv'd, and showers of oaths did melt.
I will go tell him of fair Hermia's flight;
Then to the wood will he to-morrow night
Pursue her; and for this intelligence
If I have thanks, it is a dear expense:²⁹
But herein mean I to enrich my pain,

---

²⁶ *Companies* for *companions*. So in *King Henry V.*, i. 1.: "His *companies* unletter'd, rude, and shallow."

²⁷ Here *quantity* appears to have the sense of *strength, virtue*, or *efficacy*. A like use of the word occurs in *Hamlet*, iii. 4: "Sense to ecstacy was ne'er so thrall'd, but it reserved some *quantity* of choice, to serve in such a difference."

²⁸ *Eyne*, for *eye* or *eyes*, was often used by the poets whenever that sound was wanted for the rhyme.

²⁹ The force and fitness of *expense*, here, are partly shown by *pain* in the next line. Staunton aptly notes that, as, to gratify Demetrius with this intelligence, "she makes a most painful sacrifice of her feelings, his thanks, even if obtained, are dearly bought."

To have his sight thither and back again. [*Exit.*]

SCENE II.

The Same. A Room in QUINCE'*s House.*

[*Enter* QUINCE, SNUG, BOTTOM, FLUTE, SNOUT, *and*
STARVELING.]

QUINCE. Is all our company here?

BOTTOM. You were best to call them generally, man by man,
according to the scrip.[30]

QUINCE. Here is the scroll of every man's name, which is thought fit,
through all Athens, to play in our interlude before the duke and
duchess on his wedding-day at night.

BOTTOM. First, good Peter Quince, say what the play treats on; then
read the names of the actors; and so grow to a point.

QUINCE. Marry, our play is *The most lamentable comedy and most
cruel death of Pyramus and Thisbe.*[31]

BOTTOM. A very good piece of work, I assure you, and a merry.—
Now, good Peter Quince, call forth your actors by the scroll.—
Masters, spread yourselves.

QUINCE. Answer, as I call you.—Nick Bottom, the weaver.

BOTTOM. Ready. Name what part I am for, and proceed.

QUINCE. You, Nick Bottom, are set down for Pyramus.

BOTTOM. What is Pyramus? a lover, or a tyrant?

QUINCE. A lover, that kills himself most gallantly for love.

BOTTOM. That will ask some tears in the true performing of it. If I do
it, let the audience look to their eyes; I will move storms; I will
condole in some measure. To the rest:—yet my chief humour is for
a tyrant: I could play Ercles rarely, or a part to tear a cat in, to
make all split.[32]

---

[30] *Scrip,* from *scriptum,* is *writing;* the *scroll* mentioned just below.

[31] Probably a burlesque upon the titles of some of the old dramas.

[32] *Ercles* is Bottom's version of *Hercules.* Hercules was one of the ranters and
roarers of the old moral-plays; and his Twelve Labours formed a popular subject of
entertainment. In Greene's *Groatsworth of Wit,* 1592, a player tells how he had "terribly
thundered" the Twelve Labours of Hercules. In *Histriomastix,* 1610, some soldiers drag
in a company of players; and the captain says to one of them, "Sirrah, this is you that
would rend and *tear a cat* upon the stage." And in *The Roaring Girl,* 1611, one of the
persons is called *Tear-cat.* The phrase *to make all split* is met with repeatedly. So in
Beaumont and Fletcher's *Scornful Lady,* ii. 3: "Two roaring boys of Rome, that *made all
split.*" Also in *The Widow's Tears,* by Chapman, i. 4: "Her wit I must employ upon this
business to prepare my next encounter, but in such a fashion as shall *make all split.*"

The raging rocks
And shivering shocks
Shall break the locks
Of prison gates:
And Phibbus' car
Shall shine from far,
And make and mar
The foolish Fates.

This was lofty.—Now name the rest of the players.—This is Ercles' vein, a tyrant's vein;—a lover is more condoling.

QUINCE. Francis Flute, the bellows-mender.

FLUTE. Here, Peter Quince.

QUINCE. Flute, you must take Thisbe on you.

FLUTE. What is Thisbe? a wandering knight?

QUINCE. It is the lady that Pyramus must love.

FLUTE. Nay, faith, let not me play a woman; I have a beard coming.

QUINCE. That's all one; you shall play it in a mask, and you may speak as small as you will.[33]

BOTTOM. An I may hide my face, let me play Thisbe too: I'll speak in a monstrous little voice;—*Thisne, Thisne!—Ah, Pyramus, my lover dear; thy Thisbe dear! and lady dear!*

QUINCE. No, no, you must play Pyramus; and, Flute, you Thisbe.

BOTTOM. Well, proceed.

QUINCE. Robin Starveling, the tailor.

STARVELING. Here, Peter Quince.

QUINCE. Robin Starveling, you must play Thisbe's mother.—Tom Snout, the tinker.

SNOUT. Here, Peter Quince.

QUINCE. You, Pyramus' father; myself, Thisbe's father;—Snug, the joiner, you, the lion's part:—and, I hope, here is a play fitted.

SNUG. Have you the lion's part written? pray you, if it be, give it me, for I am slow of study.

QUINCE. You may do it extempore, for it is nothing but roaring.

BOTTOM. Let me play the lion too: I will roar that I will do any man's heart good to hear me; I will roar that I will make the duke say *Let him roar again, let him roar again.*

---

[33] In *The Merry Wives*, i. 1, Slender says of Anne Page, "She has brown hair, and *speaks small* like a woman." This speech of Peter Quince's shows, what is known from other sources, that the parts of women were used to be played by boys, or, if these could not be had, by men in masks.

QUINCE. An[34] you should do it too terribly, you would fright the duchess and the ladies, that they would shriek; and that were enough to hang us all.

ALL. That would hang us every mother's son.

BOTTOM. I grant you, friends, if you should fright the ladies out of their wits, they would have no more discretion but to hang us: but I will aggravate my voice so, that I will roar you as gently as any sucking dove; I will roar you an 'twere any nightingale.

QUINCE. You can play no part but Pyramus; for Pyramus is a sweet-faced man; a proper[35] man, as one shall see in a summer's day; a most lovely gentleman-like man; therefore you must needs play Pyramus.

BOTTOM. Well, I will undertake it. What beard were I best to play it in?

QUINCE. Why, what you will.

BOTTOM. I will discharge it in either your straw-colour beard, your orange-tawny beard, your purple-in-grain beard, or your French-crown-colour beard, your perfect yellow.[36]

QUINCE. Some of your French crowns have no hair at all, and then you will play bare-faced.[37]—But, masters, here are your parts: and I am to entreat you, request you, and desire you, to con them by to-morrow night; and meet me in the palace wood, a mile without the town, by moonlight; there will we rehearse: for if we meet in the city, we shall be dogg'd with company, and our devices known. In the meantime I will draw a bill of properties,[38] such as our play wants. I pray you, fail me not.

BOTTOM. We will meet; and there we may rehearse most obscenely and courageously. Take pains; be perfect; adieu.

QUINCE. At the duke's oak we meet.

BOTTOM. Enough; hold, or cut bow-strings.[39] [*Exeunt.*]

---

[34] *An* is an old colloquial equivalent for *if.* So the Poet uses, indifferently, *an,* or *if,* or both together, *an if.* And so in the common phrase, "without any ifs or *ans.*"

[35] *Proper* is *handsome* or *fine-looking.* Commonly so in Shakespeare.

[36] It seems to have been a custom to stain or dye the beard. So Ben Jonson in *The Alchemist:* "He has *dyed his beard* and all."

[37] An allusion to the baldness attendant upon a particular stage of what was then termed the *French* disease.

[38] The *properties* were the furnishings of the stage, and the keeper of them is, I think, still called the *property-man.*

[39] This saying is no doubt rightly explained by Capell: "When a party was made at butts, assurance of meeting was given in the words of that phrase; the sense of the person using them being, that he would *hold,* or keep, his promise, or they might '*cut* his *bowstrings,*' demolish him for an archer."

ACT II.

SCENE I.

A Wood near Athens.

[*Enter, from opposite sides, a* FAIRY, *and* PUCK.]

PUCK. How now, spirit! whither wander you?
FAIRY. Over hill, over dale,
Thorough bush, thorough brier,
Over park, over pale,
Thorough flood, thorough fire,
I do wander everywhere,
Swifter than the moon's sphere;[1]
And I serve the fairy queen,
To dew her orbs[2] upon the green.
The cowslips tall her pensioners be:[3]
In their gold coats spots you see;
Those be rubies, fairy favours,
In those freckles live their savours;
I must go seek some dew-drops here,
And hang a pearl in every cowslip's ear.
Farewell, thou lob of spirits;[4] I'll be gone:

---

[1] Collier informs us that "Coleridge, in his lectures in 1818, was very emphatic in his praise of the beauty of these lines: 'the measure,' he said, 'had been invented and employed by Shakespeare for the sake of its appropriateness to the rapid and airy motion of the Fairy by whom the passage is delivered.'" And in his *Literary Remains*, after analyzing the measure, he speaks of the delightful effect on the ear," caused by "the sweet transition" from the amphimacers of the first four lines to the trochaic of the next two.

[2] These *orbs* were the verdant circles which the old superstition here delineated called fairy-rings, supposing them to be made by the night-tripping fairies dancing their merry roundels. As the ground became parched under the feet of the moonlight dancers, Puck's office was to refresh it with sprinklings of dew, thus making it greener than ever.

[3] The allusion is to Elizabeth's band of Gentleman *Pensioners*, who were chosen from among the handsomest and tallest young men of family and fortune; they were dressed in habits richly garnished with *gold lace*.

[4] It would seem that Puck, though he could "put a girdle round about the earth in forty minutes," was heavy and sluggish in comparison with the other fairies: he was the *lubber* of the spirit tribe. Shakespeare's "*lob* of spirits" is the same as Milton's "*lubbar* fiend," in *L'Allegro*:

> And he, by friar's lantern led,
> Tells how the drudging goblin swet
> To earn his cream-bowl duly set,
> When in one night, ere glimpse of morn,

Our queen and all her elves come here anon.
PUCK. The King doth keep his revels here to-night;
     Take heed the Queen come not within his sight.
     For Oberon is passing fell and wrath,
     Because that she, as her attendant, hath
     A lovely boy, stol'n from an Indian king;
     She never had so sweet a changeling:[5]
     And jealous Oberon would have the child
     Knight of his train, to trace the forests wild:
     But she perforce withholds the loved boy,
     Crowns him with flowers, and makes him all her joy:
     And now they never meet in grove or green,
     By fountain clear, or spangled starlight sheen,
     But they do square,[6] that all their elves for fear
     Creep into acorn cups, and hide them there.
FAIRY. Either I mistake your shape and making quite,
     Or else you are that shrewd and knavish sprite
     Call'd Robin Goodfellow: are not you he
     That frights the maidens of the villagery;

His shadowy flail hath thresh'd the corn,
That ten day-labourers could not end:
Then lies him down the lubbar fiend,
And, stretch'd out all the chimney's length,
Basks at the fire his hairy strength.

[5] A *changeling* was a child taken or given in *exchange*; it being a roguish custom of the fairies, if a child of great promise were born, to steal it away, and leave an ugly, or foolish, or ill-conditioned one in its stead. So in *The Faerie Queene*, i. 10, 65:

From thence a Faery thee unweeting reft,
There, as thou slepst in tender swadling band,
And her base Elfin brood there for thee left:
Such, men do *chaungelings* call, so chaung'd by Faeries theft.

How much comfort this old belief sometimes gave to parents, may be seen from Drayton's *Nymphidia*:

And when a child haps to be got,
Which after proves an idiot,
When folk perceive it thriveth not,
   The fault therein to smother,
Some silly, doating, brainless calf,
That understands things by the half,
Says that the fairy left this aulf,
   And took away the other.

[6] The Poet repeatedly uses to *square* for to *quarrel*; *squarer* for *quarreler*. This use of the word probably grew from the posture or attitude men take when they stand to a fight.

Skim milk, and sometimes labour in the quern,[7]
And bootless make the breathless housewife churn;
And sometime make the drink to bear no barm;[8]
Mislead night-wanderers, laughing at their harm?
Those that Hobgoblin call you, and sweet Puck,
You do their work, and they shall have good luck:
Are not you he?[9]
PUCK. Thou speak'st aright;
I am that merry wanderer of the night.
I jest to Oberon, and make him smile,
When I a fat and bean-fed horse beguile,
Neighing in likeness of a filly foal;[10]
And sometime lurk I in a gossip's bowl,
In very likeness of a roasted crab;[11]
And, when she drinks, against her lips I bob,
And on her withered dewlap pour the ale.
The wisest aunt,[12] telling the saddest tale,
Sometime for three-foot stool mistaketh me;
Then slip I from her bum, down topples she,
And *tailor* cries,[13] and falls into a cough;

---

[7] *Sometime* and *sometimes* were used indiscriminately.—A *quern* was a *hand-mill* for grinding corn.

[8] *Barm* is *yeast*. So in Holland's Pliny: "Now the froth or *barm*, that riseth from these ales or beers, have a property to keep the skin fair and clear in women's faces."

[9] This account of Puck was gathered from the popular notions of the time. So in Harsnet's *Declaration of Popish Impostures*: "And if that the bowl of curds and cream were not duly set out for Robin Goodfellow, the friar, and Sisse the dairy-maid, why, then either the pottage was burnt next day in the pot, or the cheeses would not curdle, or the butter would not come, or the ale in the fat never would have good head." Likewise, in Scot's *Discovery of Witchcraft*: "Your grandames' maids were wont to set a bowl of milk for him, for his pains in grinding malt and mustard, and sweeping the house at midnight;—this white bread and milk was his standing fee." And in Drayton's *Nymphidia*:

> This Puck seems but a dreaming dolt,
> Still walking like a ragged colt,
> And oft out of a bush doth bolt,
>   Of purpose to deceive us;
> And, leading us, makes us to stray
> Long winter nights out of the way,
> And when we stick in mire and clay,
>   He doth with laughter leave us.

[10] *Filly-foal* is a female colt, or a young mare. Neighing *like*, or *in the manner* of, a filly foal, is the meaning.

[11] It is the apple crab, not the animal crab, that is meant.

[12] *Aunt* and *uncle* were common titles of address to aged people; as they still are, or were of late, to aged servants in the Southern States.

And then the whole quire hold their hips and loffe,
And waxen in their mirth,[14] and neeze, and swear
A merrier hour was never wasted there.—
But room, fairy, here comes Oberon.
FAIRY. And here my mistress.—Would that he were gone!

[*Enter, from one side*, OBERON, *with his Train, from the other*
TITANIA, *with hers.*]

OBERON. Ill met by moonlight, proud Titania.
TITANIA. What, jealous Oberon?—Fairies, skip hence;
I have forsworn his bed and company.
OBERON. Tarry, rash wanton: am not I thy lord?
TITANIA. Then I must be thy lady; but I know
When thou hast stol'n away from fairy-land,
And in the shape of Corin sat all day,
Playing on pipes of corn,[15] and versing love
To amorous Phillida. Why art thou here,
Come from the farthest steep of India,
But that, forsooth, the bouncing Amazon,
Your buskin'd mistress and your warrior love,
To Theseus must be wedded; and you come
To give their bed joy and prosperity.
OBERON. How canst thou thus, for shame, Titania,
Glance at my credit with Hippolyta,
Knowing I know thy love to Theseus?
Didst not thou lead him through the glimmering night
From Perigenia, whom he ravish'd?
And make him with fair Aegles break his faith,
With Ariadne and Antiopa?
TITANIA. These are the forgeries of jealousy:
And never, since the middle Summer's spring,[16]
Met we on hill, in dale, forest, or mead,
By paved fountain, or by rushy brook,

---

[13] Dr. Johnson thought he remembered to have heard this ludicrous exclamation
upon a person's seat slipping from under him. He that slips from his chair falls as a *tailor*
squats upon his board.
[14] *Waxen* is an old plural form of the verb to *wax*. Of course it means "*increase*" in
their mirth."
[15] A *pipe of corn* is an ancient musical instrument, made of the straw of wheat, oats,
or rye; straws of different size being selected, and cut of different lengths, and then
fastened together in a small frame or holder. Such was the shepherd's pipe, though
sometimes made of reeds, so much celebrated in classic poetry.
[16] *Spring* is here used in the sense of *beginning*. The Poet has elsewhere "*spring* of
day" in the same sense. So in Job xxxviii. 12: "Hast thou caused the *day-spring* to know
his place?"

Or on the beached margent of the sea,
To dance our ringlets to the whistling wind,
But with thy brawls thou hast disturb'd our sport.
Therefore the winds, piping to us in vain,
As in revenge, have suck'd up from the sea
Contagious fogs; which, falling in the land,
Hath every pelting[17] river made so proud
That they have overborne their continents:[18]
The ox hath therefore stretch'd his yoke in vain,
The ploughman lost his sweat; and the green corn
Hath rotted ere his youth attain'd a beard:
The fold stands empty in the drowned field,
And crows are fatted with the murrion flock;
The nine men's morris[19] is fill'd up with mud;
And the quaint mazes in the wanton green,
For lack of tread, are undistinguishable:
The human mortals want[20] their winter here;
No night is now with hymn or carol blest:—
Therefore the moon, the governess of floods,
Pale in her anger, washes all the air,
That rheumatic diseases do abound:
And thorough this distemperature we see
The seasons alter: hoary-headed frosts
Fall in the fresh lap of the crimson rose;
And on old Hiem's thin and icy crown
An odorous chaplet of sweet summer buds

---

[17] *Pelting* was often used for *petty* or *paltry*.

[18] *Continent* was formerly used of that which *contains* anything; as a river is contained within its banks.

[19] This was a plat of green turf cut into a sort of chess board, for the rustic youth to exercise their skill upon. The game was called nine-men's-morris, because the players had each nine men, which they moved along the lines cut in the ground, until one side had taken or penned up all those on the other. "The quaint mazes in the wanton green" were where the youths and maidens led their happy dances in the open air.

[20] To *want* was not unfrequently used in the sense of to *lack*, or to *be* without.—All through this speech the Poet probably had in mind the Summer of 1594, which was much celebrated for the strange misbehaviour of the weather. So in Dr. Forman's *Diary*: "This monethes of June and July were very wet and wonderful cold, like winter, that the 10 dae of Julii many did syt by the fyer, yt was so cold; and soe was it in Maye and June; and scarse too fair dais all that tyme, but it rayned every day more or lesse." Also in Churchyard's poem, *Charitie*, published in 1595:

A colder time in world was never seen:
The skies do lour, the sun and moon wax dim;
Summer scarce known, but that the leaves are green:
The winter's waste drives water o'er the brim; &c.

Is, as in mockery, set: the spring, the summer,
The childing[21] autumn, angry winter, change
Their wonted liveries; and the maz'd world,
By their increase, now knows not which is which:
And this same progeny of evils comes
From our debate, from our dissension:
We are their parents and original.
OBERON. Do you amend it, then: it lies in you:
Why should Titania cross her Oberon?
I do but beg a little changeling boy
To be my henchman.[22]
TITANIA. Set your heart at rest;
The fairy-land buys not the child of me.
His mother was a vot'ress of my order:
And, in the spiced Indian air, by night,
Full often hath she gossip'd by my side;
And sat with me on Neptune's yellow sands,
Marking the embarked traders on the flood;
When we have laugh'd to see the sails conceive,
And grow big-bellied with the wanton wind;
Which she, with pretty and with swimming gait
Following,—her womb then rich with my young squire,—
Would imitate; and sail upon the land,
To fetch me trifles, and return again,
As from a voyage, rich with merchandise.
But she, being mortal, of that boy did die;
And for her sake do I rear up her boy:
And for her sake I will not part with him.
OBERON. How long within this wood intend you stay?
TITANIA. Perchance till after Theseus' wedding-day.
If you will patiently dance in our round,
And see our moonlight revels, go with us;
If not, shun me, and I will spare your haunts.
OBERON. Give me that boy and I will go with thee.
TITANIA. Not for thy fairy kingdom. Fairies, away:
We shall chide downright if I longer stay.

[*Exit* TITANIA *with her Train.*]

---

[21] *Childing*, here, is *teeming* or *fruitful*. In the second line below, *their increase* is
the *produce* of the several seasons, which is supposed to have become so mixed and
confounded, that mankind are *bewildered*, or *in a maze*. This use of *childing* and *increase*
is well illustrated in the Poet's 97th Sonnet: "The *teeming* Autumn, big with rich
increase, bearing the wanton burden of the prime," &c.

[22] *Henchman* is an *attendant* or *page*; probably from the Saxon *hengst*, a *groom*.

OBERON. Well, go thy way: thou shalt not from this grove
    Till I torment thee for this injury.—
    My gentle Puck, come hither: thou remember'st
    Since[23] once I sat upon a promontory,
    And heard a mermaid,[24] on a dolphin's back,
    Uttering such dulcet and harmonious breath,
    That the rude sea grew civil at her song,
    And certain stars shot madly from their spheres
    To hear[25] the sea-maid's music.
PUCK. I remember.
OBERON. That very time I saw,—but thou couldst not,—
    Flying between the cold moon and the earth,
    Cupid, all arm'd: a certain aim he took
    At a fair vestal, throned by the west;
    And loos'd his love-shaft smartly from his bow,
    As it should pierce a hundred thousand hearts;
    But I might see young Cupid's fiery shaft
    Quench'd in the chaste beams of the watery moon;
    And the imperial votress passed on,
    In maiden meditation, fancy-free.[26]
    Yet mark'd I where the bolt of Cupid fell:
    It fell upon a little western flower,—
    Before milk-white, now purple with love's wound,—
    And maidens call it love-in-idleness.[27]
    Fetch me that flower, the herb I showed thee once:
    The juice of it on sleeping eyelids laid
    Will make or man or woman madly dote
    Upon the next live creature that it sees.
    Fetch me this herb: and be thou here again
    Ere the leviathan can swim a league.
PUCK. I'll put a girdle round about the earth
    In forty minutes. [*Exit.*]
OBERON. Having once this juice,

---

[23] *Since* was sometimes used for *when*; and such is clearly the sense of it here. So in *2 Henry IV.*, iii. 2: "Do you remember *since* we lay all night in the windmill in Saint George's fields?"

[24] In Shakespeare's time, *mermaid* appears to have been sometimes used for *siren.*

[25] *To hear* is an instance of what is called the gerundial infinitive, and so is equivalent to *at hearing*; the hearing of the seamaid's music being assigned, not as the *purpose*, but as the *cause* of the stars shooting madly from their spheres.

[26] This delectable passage is universally understood as a compliment to Queen Elizabeth.

[27] The tri-coloured violet, commonly called pansies, or hearts-ease, is here meant: one or two of its petals are of a purple colour. It has other fanciful and expressive names, such as Cuddle-me-to-you, Three-faces-under-a-hood, Herb-trinity, &c.

I'll watch Titania when she is asleep,
And drop the liquor of it in her eyes:
The next thing then she waking looks upon,—
Be it on lion, bear, or wolf, or bull,
On meddling monkey, or on busy ape,—
She shall pursue it with the soul of love.
And ere I take this charm from off her sight,—
As I can take it with another herb,
I'll make her render up her page to me.
But who comes here? I am invisible;
And I will overhear their conference.

[*Enter* DEMETRIUS, HELENA *following him.*]

DEMETRIUS. I love thee not, therefore pursue me not.
Where is Lysander and fair Hermia?
The one I'll slay, the other slayeth me.
Thou told'st me they were stol'n into this wood,
And here am I, and wood[28] within this wood,
Because I cannot meet with Hermia.
Hence, get thee gone, and follow me no more.
HELENA. You draw me, you hard-hearted adamant;[29]
But yet you draw not iron, for my heart
Is true as steel. Leave you your power to draw,
And I shall have no power to follow you.
DEMETRIUS. Do I entice you? Do I speak you fair?
Or, rather, do I not in plainest truth
Tell you I do not, nor I cannot love you?
HELENA. And even for that do I love you the more.
I am your spaniel; and, Demetrius,
The more you beat me, I will fawn on you:
Use me but as your spaniel, spurn me, strike me,
Neglect me, lose me; only give me leave,
Unworthy as I am, to follow you.
What worser place can I beg in your love,
And yet a place of high respect with me,—
Than to be used as you use your dog?
DEMETRIUS. Tempt not too much the hatred of my spirit;
For I am sick when I do look on thee.

---

[28] *Wood* is an old word for *frantic* or *mad.*
[29] "There is now a dayes a kind of *adamant* which draweth unto it fleshe, and the same so strongly, that it hath power to knit and tie together two mouthes of contrary persons, and drawe the heart of a man out of his bodie without offending any part of him."—*Certaine Secrete Wonders of Nature*, by Edward Fenton, 1569.

HELENA. And I am sick when I look not on you.
DEMETRIUS. You do impeach your modesty too much,
    To leave the city, and commit yourself
    Into the hands of one that loves you not;
    To trust the opportunity of night,
    And the ill counsel of a desert place,
    With the rich worth of your virginity.
HELENA. Your virtue is my privilege for that.
    It is not night when I do see your face,
    Therefore I think I am not in the night;
    Nor doth this wood lack worlds of company;
    For you, in my respect, are all the world:
    Then how can it be said I am alone
    When all the world is here to look on me?
DEMETRIUS. I'll run from thee, and hide me in the brakes,
    And leave thee to the mercy of wild beasts.
HELENA. The wildest hath not such a heart as you.
    Run when you will, the story shall be chang'd;
    Apollo flies, and Daphne holds the chase;
    The dove pursues the griffin; the mild hind
    Makes speed to catch the tiger,—bootless speed,
    When cowardice pursues and valour flies.
DEMETRIUS. I will not stay thy question;[30] let me go:
    Or, if thou follow me, do not believe
    But I shall do thee mischief in the wood.
HELENA. Ay, in the temple, in the town, the field,
    You do me mischief. Fie, Demetrius!
    Your wrongs do set a scandal on my sex:
    We cannot fight for love as men may do:
    We should be woo'd, and were not made to woo.
    I'll follow thee, and make a heaven of hell,
    To die upon the hand I love so well.

[*Exeunt* DEMETRIUS *and* HELENA.]

OBERON. Fare thee well, nymph: ere he do leave this grove,
    Thou shalt fly him, and he shall seek thy love.—

[*Re-enter* PUCK.]

    Hast thou the flower there? Welcome, wanderer.
PUCK. Ay, there it is.

---

[30] Here, as often, *question* is *talk* or *conversation*.

OBERON. I pray thee give it me.
 I know a bank whereon the wild thyme blows,
 Where ox-lips and the nodding violet grows;
 Quite over-canopied with lush[31] woodbine,
 With sweet musk-roses, and with eglantine:
 There sleeps Titania sometime of the night,
 Lulled in these flowers with dances and delight;
 And there the snake throws her enamell'd skin,
 Weed wide enough to wrap a fairy in:
 And with the juice of this I'll streak her eyes,
 And make her full of hateful fantasies.
 Take thou some of it, and seek through this grove:
 A sweet Athenian lady is in love
 With a disdainful youth: anoint his eyes;
 But do it when the next thing he espies
 May be the lady: thou shalt know the man
 By the Athenian garments he hath on.
 Effect it with some care, that he may prove
 More fond on her than she upon her love:
 And look thou meet me ere the first cock crow.
PUCK. Fear not, my lord; your servant shall do so. [*Exeunt.*]

SCENE II.

Another part of the wood.

[*Enter* TITANIA, *with her Train.*]

TITANIA. Come, now a roundel[32] and a fairy song;
 Then, for the third part of a minute, hence;
 Some to kill cankers in the musk-rose buds;
 Some war with rere-mice[33] for their leathern wings,
 To make my small elves coats; and some keep back
 The clamorous owl, that nightly hoots and wonders
 At our quaint[34] spirits. Sing me now asleep;
 Then to your offices, and let me rest.

---

[31] *Lush* is *luscious* or *luxuriant.* So in *The Tempest,* ii. i: "How *lush* and lusty the grass looks! how green!"

[32] *Roundel* was the name of a *dance* in which the parties joined hands and formed a ring; sometimes called a *roundelay.*

[33] *Rere-mice* is an old name for *bats.*

[34] *Quaint* is *ingenious, adroit, cunning.*

SONG.

1 FAIRY.	*You spotted snakes, with double tongue,*
	Thorny hedgehogs, be not seen;
	Newts and blind-worms,[35] *do no wrong;*
	Come not near our fairy queen:
CHORUS.	*Philomel, with melody,*
	Sing in our sweet lullaby:
	Lulla, lulla, lullaby; lulla, lulla, lullaby:
	Never harm, nor spell, nor charm,
	Come our lovely lady nigh;
	So good-night, with lullaby.
2 FAIRY.	*Weaving spiders, come not here;*
	Hence, you long-legg'd spinners, hence;
	Beetles black, approach not near;
	Worm nor snail do no offence.
CHORUS.	*Philomel with melody, &c.*
1 FAIRY.	Hence away; now all is well.
	One, aloof, stand sentinel.

[*Exeunt Fairies.* TITANIA *sleeps.*]

[*Enter* OBERON.]

OBERON. What thou seest when thou dost wake,

[*Squeezes the flower on* TITANIA'*s eyelids.*]

Do it for thy true-love take;
Love and languish for his sake;
Be it ounce, or cat, or bear,
Pard,[36] or boar with bristled hair,
In thy eye that shall appear
When thou wak'st, it is thy dear;
Wake when some vile thing is near. [*Exit.*]

[*Enter* LYSANDER *and* HERMIA.]

LYSANDER. Fair love, you faint with wandering in the wood;
And, to speak troth, I have forgot our way;

---

[35] The *blind-worm* is what is now called the *slow-worm*. It is, I believe, quite harmless, but did not use to be thought so.

[36] *Pard* is an old name for *leopard.*

We'll rest us, Hermia, if you think it good,
And tarry for the comfort of the day.
HERMIA. Be it so, Lysander: find you out a bed,
For I upon this bank will rest my head.
LYSANDER. One turf shall serve as pillow for us both;
One heart, one bed, two bosoms, and one troth.
HERMIA. Nay, good Lysander; for my sake, my dear,
Lie farther off yet, do not lie so near.
LYSANDER. O, take the sense, sweet, of my innocence![37]
Love takes the meaning in love's conference.
I mean that my heart unto yours is knit;
So that but one heart we can make of it:
Two bosoms interchained with an oath;
So then two bosoms and a single troth.
Then by your side no bed-room me deny;
For lying so, Hermia, I do not lie.
HERMIA. Lysander riddles very prettily:—
Now much beshrew my manners and my pride
If Hermia meant to say Lysander lied!
But, gentle friend, for love and courtesy
Lie further off; in human modesty,
Such separation as may well be said
Becomes a virtuous bachelor and a maid:
So far be distant; and good night, sweet friend:
Thy love ne'er alter till thy sweet life end!
LYSANDER. Amen, amen, to that fair prayer say I;
And then end life when I end loyalty!
Here is my bed: Sleep give thee all his rest!
HERMIA. With half that wish the wisher's eyes be pressed!

[*They sleep.*]

[*Enter* PUCK.]

PUCK.   Through the forest have I gone,
                    But Athenian found I none,
                    On whose eyes I might approve
                    This flower's force in stirring love.
                    Night and silence! Who is here?
                    Weeds of Athens he doth wear:
                    This is he, my master said,
                    Despised the Athenian maid;

---

[37] That is, "understand the meaning of my innocence," or "my innocent meaning."

And here the maiden, sleeping sound,
On the dank and dirty ground.
Pretty soul! she durst not lie
Near this lack-love, this kill-courtesy.
Churl, upon thy eyes I throw
All the power this charm doth owe.[38]

[*Squeezes the flower on* LYSANDER's *eyelids.*]

When thou wak'st let love forbid
Sleep his seat on thy eyelid:
So awake when I am gone;
For I must now to Oberon.

[*Enter* DEMETRIUS *and* HELENA, *running.*]

HELENA. Stay, though thou kill me, sweet Demetrius.
DEMETRIUS. I charge thee, hence, and do not haunt me thus.
HELENA. O, wilt thou darkling leave me?[39] do not so.
DEMETRIUS. Stay on thy peril; I alone will go. [*Exit.*]
HELENA. O, I am out of breath in this fond chase!
The more my prayer, the lesser is my grace.
Happy is Hermia, wheresoe'er she lies,
For she hath blessed and attractive eyes.
How came her eyes so bright? Not with salt tears:
If so, my eyes are oftener wash'd than hers.
No, no, I am as ugly as a bear;
For beasts that meet me run away for fear:
Therefore no marvel though Demetrius
Do, as a monster, fly my presence thus.
What wicked and dissembling glass of mine
Made me compare with Hermia's sphery eyne?—
But who is here?—Lysander! on the ground!
Dead? or asleep? I see no blood, no wound.
Lysander, if you live, good sir, awake.
LYSANDER [*Starting up.*] And run through fire I will for thy sweet
sake.
Transparent Helena! Nature shows art,
That through thy bosom makes me see thy heart.
Where is Demetrius? O, how fit a word
Is that vile name to perish on my sword!

---

[38] *Owe* is continually used by the old poets for *own* or *possess.*
[39] An old phrase, meaning, "wilt thou leave me *in the dark?*" So in *King Lear*, i.4:
"So, out went the candle, and we were left *darkling.*"

HELENA. Do not say so, Lysander; say not so:
    What though he love your Hermia? Lord, what though?
    Yet Hermia still loves you: then be content.
LYSANDER. Content with Hermia? No: I do repent
    The tedious minutes I with her have spent.
    Not Hermia but Helena I love:
    Who will not change a raven for a dove?
    The will of man is by his reason sway'd;
    And reason says you are the worthier maid.
    Things growing are not ripe until their season;
    So I, being young, till now ripe not to reason;
    And touching now the point of human skill,
    Reason becomes the marshal to my will,
    And leads me to your eyes, where I o'erlook
    Love's stories, written in love's richest book.
HELENA. Wherefore was I to this keen mockery born?
    When at your hands did I deserve this scorn?
    Is't not enough, is't not enough, young man,
    That I did never, no, nor never can
    Deserve a sweet look from Demetrius' eye,
    But you must flout my insufficiency?
    Good troth, you do me wrong,—good sooth, you do—
    In such disdainful manner me to woo.
    But fare you well: perforce I must confess,
    I thought you lord of more true gentleness.
    O, that a lady of one man refus'd
    Should of another therefore be abused! [*Exit.*]
LYSANDER. She sees not Hermia:—Hermia, sleep thou there;
    And never mayst thou come Lysander near!
    For, as a surfeit of the sweetest things
    The deepest loathing to the stomach brings;
    Or, as the heresies that men do leave
    Are hated most of those they did deceive;
    So thou, my surfeit and my heresy,
    Of all be hated, but the most of me!
    And, all my powers, address your love and might
    To honour Helen, and to be her knight! [*Exit.*]
HERMIA. [*Starting.*] Help me, Lysander, help me! do thy best
    To pluck this crawling serpent from my breast!
    Ay me, for pity!—What a dream was here!
    Lysander, look how I do quake with fear!
    Methought a serpent eat my heart away,
    And you sat smiling at his cruel prey.—
    Lysander! what, removed? Lysander! lord!
    What, out of hearing? gone? no sound, no word?

Alack, where are you? speak, an if you hear;
Speak, of all loves![40] I swoon almost with fear.
No?—then I well perceive you are not nigh:
Either death or you I'll find immediately. [*Exit.*]

---

[40] A petty adjuration of the time, equivalent to *by all means.*

ACT III.

SCENE I.

The Wood. TITANIA *lying asleep.*

[*Enter* QUINCE, SNUG, BOTTOM, FLUTE, SNOUT, *and*
STARVELING.]

BOTTOM. Are we all met?

QUINCE. Pat, pat; and here's a marvellous convenient place for our
rehearsal. This green plot shall be our stage, this hawthorn brake
our tiring-house; and we will do it in action, as we will do it before
the duke.

BOTTOM. Peter Quince,—

QUINCE. What sayest thou, bully Bottom?

BOTTOM. There are things in this comedy of *Pyramus and Thisbe* that
will never please. First, Pyramus must draw a sword to kill
himself; which the ladies cannot abide. How answer you that?

SNOUT. By'r lakin, a parlous fear.[1]

STARVELING. I believe we must leave the killing out, when all is
done.

BOTTOM. Not a whit: I have a device to make all well. Write me a
prologue; and let the prologue seem to say we will do no harm
with our swords, and that Pyramus is not killed indeed; and for the
more better assurance, tell them that I Pyramus am not Pyramus
but Bottom the weaver: this will put them out of fear.

QUINCE. Well, we will have such a prologue; and it shall be written in
eight and six.[2]

BOTTOM. No, make it two more; let it be written in eight and eight.

SNOUT. Will not the ladies be afeard of the lion?

STARVELING. I fear it, I promise you.

BOTTOM. Masters, you ought to consider with yourselves: to bring in,
God shield us! a lion among ladies is a most dreadful thing: for
there is not a more fearful wild-fowl than your lion living; and we
ought to look to it.

SNOUT. Therefore another prologue must tell he is not a lion.

BOTTOM. Nay, you must name his name, and half his face must be
seen through the lion's neck; and he himself must speak through,

---

[1] *By'r lakin* is a diminutive of *by'r Lady*, which, again, is a contraction of *by our
Lady*, an old oath of frequent occurrence in these plays; *Lady* meaning the Virgin Mary.
Parlous is a corruption of *perilous.*

[2] In alternate verses of eight and six syllables.

saying thus, or to the same defect,—*Ladies,*—or,—*Fair ladies,*—*I would wish you,*—or,—*I would request you,*—or,—*I would entreat you,*—*not to fear, not to tremble: my life for yours. If you think I come hither as a lion, it were pity of my life. No, I am no such thing*; *I am a man as other men are:*—and there, indeed, let him name his name, and tell them plainly he is Snug the joiner.³

QUINCE. Well, it shall be so. But there is two hard things; that is, to bring the moonlight into a chamber: for, you know, Pyramus and Thisbe meet by moonlight.

SNOUT. Doth the moon shine that night we play our play?

BOTTOM. A calendar, a calendar! look in the almanac; find out moonshine, find out moonshine.

QUINCE. Yes, it doth shine that night.

BOTTOM. Why, then may you leave a casement of the great chamber-window, where we play, open; and the moon may shine in at the casement.

QUINCE. Ay; or else one must come in with a bush of thorns and a lantern, and say he comes to disfigure or to present the person of moonshine. Then there is another thing: we must have a wall in the great chamber; for Pyramus and Thisbe, says the story, did talk through the chink of a wall.

SNOUT. You can never bring in a wall.—What say you, Bottom?

BOTTOM. Some man or other must present wall: and let him have some plaster, or some loam, or some rough-cast about him, to signify wall; and let him hold his fingers thus, and through that cranny shall Pyramus and Thisbe whisper.

QUINCE. If that may be, then all is well. Come, sit down, every mother's son, and rehearse your parts. Pyramus, you begin: when you have spoken your speech, enter into that brake; and so every one according to his cue.

[*Enter* PUCK *behind.*]

PUCK. What hempen homespuns have we swaggering here,
So near the cradle of the fairy queen?

---

³ Shakespeare may here allude to an incident said to have occurred in his time, which is recorded in a collection entitled *Merry Passages and Jests*: "There was a spectacle presented to Queen Elizabeth upon the water, and among others Harry Goldingham was to represent Arion upon the Dolphin's backe; but finding his voice to be verye hoarse and unpleasant when he came to perform it, he tears off his disguise, and swears he was none of Arion, not he, but even honest Harry Goldenham; which blunt discoverie pleased the queen better than if he had gone through in the right way:—yet he could order his voice to an instrument exceeding well."

What, a play toward![4] I'll be an auditor;
An actor too perhaps, if I see cause.
QUINCE. Speak, Pyramus.—Thisbe, stand forth.
PYRAMUS. *Thisbe, the flowers of odious savours sweet,*
QUINCE. *Odours, odours.*
PYRAMUS.—*odours savours sweet:*
So hath thy breath, my dearest Thisbe dear.
But hark, a voice! stay thou but here awhile,
And by and by I will to thee appear. [*Exit.*]
PUCK. [*Aside.*] A stranger Pyramus than e'er played here!

[*Exit.*]

FLUTE. Must I speak now?
QUINCE. Ay, marry, must you: for you must understand he goes but to
see a noise that he heard, and is to come again.
THISBE. *Most radiant Pyramus, most lily white of hue,*
Of colour like the red rose on triumphant brier,
Most brisky juvenal,[5] *and eke most lovely Jew,*
As true as truest horse, that would never tire,
I'll meet thee, Pyramus, at Ninny's tomb.
QUINCE. *Ninus'* tomb, man: why, you must not speak that yet: that
you answer to Pyramus. You speak all your part at once, cues[6] and
all.—Pyramus enter: your cue is past; it is *never tire.*
THISBE. O,—*As true as truest horse, that yet would never tire.*

[*Re-enter* PUCK, *and* BOTTOM *with an ass's head.*]

PYRAMUS. *If I were fair, Thisbe, I were only thine:*—
QUINCE.O monstrous! O strange! we are haunted.—Pray, masters!
fly, masters!—Help!

[*Exit with* SNUG, FLUTE, SNOUT, *and* STARVELING.]

PUCK. I'll follow you; I'll lead you about a round,
Through bog, through bush, through brake, through briar;
Sometime a horse I'll be, sometime a hound,
A hog, a headless bear, sometime a fire;
And neigh, and bark, and grunt, and roar, and burn,

---

[4] *Toward*, here, is *at hand, in hand,* or *forthcoming.* Very often used so by the Poet.
Nor is the usage altogether out of date now.
[5] *Juvenal* is *youth*; so used several times by Shakespeare.
[6] The *cues* were the last words of the preceding speech, which served as a hint to
him who was to speak next.

Like horse, hound, hog, bear, fire, at every turn.[7] [*Exit.*]
BOTTOM. Why do they run away? This is a knavery of them to make
me afeard.

[*Re-enter* SNOUT.]

SNOUT. O Bottom, thou art changed! What do I see on thee?
BOTTOM. What do you see? you see an ass-head of your own, do
you? [*Exit* SNOUT.]

[*Re-enter* QUINCE.]

QUINCE. Bless thee, Bottom! bless thee! thou art translated. [*Exit.*]
BOTTOM. I see their knavery: this is to make an ass of me; to fright
me, if they could. But I will not stir from this place, do what they
can: I will walk up and down here, and I will sing, that they shall
hear I am not afraid.

[*Sings.*]

> *The ousel cock, so black of hue,*
> *With orange-tawny bill,[8]*
> *The throstle with his note so true,*
> *The wren with little quill.*

TITANIA. [*Awaking.*] What angel wakes me from my flowery bed?

---

[7] The Protean versatility of Puck is celebrated in whatsoever has come down to us
respecting him. Thus in an old tract entitled *Robin Goodfellow, his Mad Pranks and
Merry Jests*:

> Thou hast the power to change thy shape
> To horse, to hog, to dog, to ape.

[8] In the opinion of some commentators, the Poet or Bottom is a little out here in his
ornithology. This opinion has probably arisen from a change in the use of the name since
Shakespeare's day; *ousel* being then used to denote the *blackbird.* Bottom's *orange-
tawny* bill accords with what Yarrel says of the blackbird: "The beak and the edges of the
eyelids in the adult male are *gamboge yellow.*" The *whistling* of the blackbird is thus
noted in Spenser's *Epithalamion*:

> The merry Larke hir mattins sings aloft;
> The Thrush replyes; the Mavis descant playes;
> The *Ouzell shrills*; the Ruddock warbles soft.

BOTTOM. [*Sings.*]

> *The finch, the sparrow, and the lark,*
> *The plain-song cuckoo*[9] *gray,*
> *Whose note full many a man doth mark,*
> *And dares not answer nay;—*

for, indeed, who would set his wit to so foolish a bird?
Who would give a bird the lie, though he cry *cuckoo* never so?[10]
TITANIA. I pray thee, gentle mortal, sing again;
Mine ear is much enamour'd of thy note.
So is mine eye enthralled to thy shape;
And thy fair virtue's force perforce doth move me,
On the first view, to say, to swear, I love thee.
BOTTOM. Methinks, mistress, you should have little reason for that:
and yet, to say the truth, reason and love keep little company
together now-a-days: the more the pity that some honest
neighbours will not make them friends. Nay, I can gleek[11] upon
occasion.
TITANIA. Thou art as wise as thou art beautiful.
BOTTOM. Not so, neither: but if I had wit[12] enough to get out of this
wood, I have enough to serve mine own turn.
TITANIA. Out of this wood do not desire to go;
Thou shalt remain here whether thou wilt or no.
I am a spirit of no common rate,—
The summer still doth tend upon my state;
And I do love thee: therefore, go with me,
I'll give thee fairies to attend on thee;
And they shall fetch thee jewels from the deep,
And sing, while thou on pressed flowers dost sleep:
And I will purge thy mortal grossness so
That thou shalt like an airy spirit go.—
Peas-blossom! Cobweb! Moth! and Mustardseed!

---

[9] The cuckoo is called *plain-song*, as having no variety of note, but singing in a monotone, after the manner of the ancient simple *chant*.

[10] "Set his wit to a bird" is *contradict, argue with*, or *match himself against* a bird. In *Troilus and Cressida*, ii. 1, Achilles says to Ajax, "Will you *set your wit* to a fool's?" and Thersites replies, "No, I warrant you; for a fool's will shame it."—"Though he cry *cuckoo*" refers to the likeness of sound in *cuckoo* and *cuckold*. So in the song at the end of *Love's Labours Lost*: "*Cuckoo, cuckoo,*—O word of fear, unpleasing to a married ear!"

[11] Bottom is chuckling over the wit he has just vented. *Gleek* is from the Anglo-Saxon *glig*, and means *catch, entrap, play upon, scoff at*. So says Richardson. *Glee* is from the same original.

[12] This is one instance out of many in these plays, showing that *wit* and *wisdom* were used as equivalents.

[*Enter* PEAS-BLOSSOM, COBWEB, MOTH, *and*
   MUSTARDSEED.]

PEAS-BLOSSOM. Ready.
COBWEB. And I.
MOTH. And I.
MUSTARDSEED. And I.
ALL. Where shall we go?
TITANIA. Be kind and courteous to this gentleman;
   Hop in his walks and gambol in his eyes;
   Feed him with apricocks and dewberries,
   With purple grapes, green figs, and mulberries;
   The honey bags steal from the humble-bees,[13]
   And, for night-tapers, crop their waxen thighs,
   And light them at the fiery glow-worm's eyes,
   To have my love to bed and to arise;
   And pluck the wings from painted butterflies,
   To fan the moonbeams from his sleeping eyes:
   Nod to him, elves, and do him courtesies.
PEAS-BLOSSOM. Hail, mortal!
COBWEB. Hail!
MOTH. Hail!
MUSTARDSEED. Hail!
BOTTOM. I cry your worships mercy[14] heartily.—I beseech your
   worship's name.
COBWEB. Cobweb.
BOTTOM. I shall desire you of more acquaintance,[15] good Master
   Cobweb. If I cut my finger, I shall make bold with you.—Your
   name, honest gentleman?
PEAS-BLOSSOM. Peas-blossom.
BOTTOM. I pray you, commend me to Mistress Squash,[16] your
   mother, and to Master Peascod, your father. Good Master Peas-
   blossom, I shall desire you of more acquaintance too.—Your
   name, I beseech you, sir?
MUSTARDSEED. Mustardseed.
BOTTOM. Good Master Mustardseed, I know your patience well:[17]

---

[13] What we call *bumble-bees*; so called from their loud *humming*.
[14] "I cry you mercy" is an old phrase for "I ask your pardon."
[15] A common form of speech in the Poet's time. So in *The Merchant*, iv. 1: "I
humbly do desire your *Grace of pardon.*"
[16] *Squash* seems to have been originally used of such immature vegetables as were
eaten in the state of immaturity. In Shakespeare's time, the word had got appropriated to
an immature peascod. When or how it came to its present meaning I cannot say.
[17] Bottom here seems rather too deep for the editors. Does he mean "your patience"
in suffering "that same cowardly, giant-like ox-beef" to devour "many a gentleman of

That same cowardly giant-like ox-beef hath devoured many a
gentleman of your house: I promise you your kindred hath made
my eyes water ere now. I desire you of more acquaintance, good
Master Mustardseed.

TITANIA. Come, wait upon him; lead him to my bower.
The moon, methinks, looks with a watery eye;
And when she weeps, weeps every little flower;
Lamenting some enforced chastity.
Tie up my love's tongue, bring him silently. [*Exeunt.*]

SCENE II.

Another Part of the Wood.

[*Enter* OBERON.]

OBERON. I wonder if Titania be awak'd;
Then, what it was that next came in her eye,
Which she must dote on in extremity.
Here comes my messenger.—

[*Enter* PUCK.]

How now, mad spirit?
What night-rule[18] now about this haunted grove?
PUCK. My mistress with a monster is in love.
Near to her close and consecrated bower,
While she was in her dull and sleeping hour,
A crew of patches,[19] rude mechanicals,
That work for bread upon Athenian stalls,
Were met together to rehearse a play
Intended for great Theseus' nuptial day.
The shallowest thickskin of that barren sort,[20]
Who Pyramus presented in their sport,
Forsook his scene and enter'd in a brake;
When I did him at this advantage take,

---

your House"? It has been proposed to read "*passing* well"; but this might be a parlous
defeature of Bottom's idiom.
    [18] *Night-rule* is such rule as is apt to govern in the *night; revelry.*
    [19] This use of *patch* is said to have grown from the motley or *patch-work* dress worn
by the "allowed Fool." At all events, it came to be used generally as a term of contempt
for a simpleton or a clown. Shakespeare has it repeatedly in that sense.
    [20] *Sort* here means *pack,* or *company;* the same as *crew,* a little before. The Poet has
several instances of such use; as, "a *sort* of traitors," and "a *sort* of tinkers," and "a *sort*
of vagabonds." "Many in a *sort*" a little after, is another instance.

An ass's nowl[21] I fixed on his head;
Anon, his Thisbe must be answered,
And forth my mimic comes. When they him spy,
As wild geese that the creeping fowler eye,
Or russet-pated choughs,[22] many in sort,
Rising and cawing at the gun's report,
Sever themselves and madly sweep the sky,
So at his sight away his fellows fly:
And at our stamp here, o'er and o'er one falls;
He *murder* cries, and help from Athens calls.
Their sense thus weak, lost with their fears, thus strong,
Made senseless things begin to do them wrong;
For briers and thorns at their apparel snatch;
Some sleeves, some hats: from yielders all things catch.
I led them on in this distracted[23] fear,
And left sweet Pyramus translated there:
When in that moment,—so it came to pass,—
Titania wak'd, and straightway lov'd an ass.
OBERON. This falls out better than I could devise.
But hast thou yet latch'd[24] the Athenian's eyes
With the love-juice, as I did bid thee do?
PUCK. I took him sleeping,—that is finish'd too,—
And the Athenian woman by his side;
That, when he wak'd, of force she must be ey'd.

[*Enter* HERMIA *and* DEMETRIUS.]

OBERON. Stand close; this is the same Athenian.
PUCK. This is the woman, but not this the man.
DEMETRIUS. O, why rebuke you him that loves you so?
Lay breath so bitter on your bitter foe.
HERMIA. Now I but chide, but I should use thee worse;
For thou, I fear, hast given me cause to curse.
If thou hast slain Lysander in his sleep,
Being o'er shoes in blood, plunge in the deep,
And kill me too.
The sun was not so true unto the day

---

[21] *Nowl* is an old word for *head.* Perhaps it is but a special application of *knoll*; that use growing from the rounded shape of what we now mean by that word.

[22] Yarrell, in his *History of British Birds*, says that Shakespeare here "speaks of the russet-pated (grey-headed) Choughs; which term is applicable to the Jackdaw, but not the real Choughs."

[23] *Distracted* for *distracting*; the passive form with the active tense. See page 16, note 5.

[24] *Latch'd*, or *letch'd*, is *licked* or *smeared over.* From the French *lecher.*

As he to me: would he have stol'n away
From sleeping Hermia? I'll believe as soon
This whole earth may be bor'd; and that the moon
May through the centre creep and so displease
Her brother's noontide with the antipodes.
It cannot be but thou hast murder'd him;
So should a murderer look; so dead, so grim.
DEMETRIUS. So should the murder'd look; and so should I,
Pierc'd through the heart with your stern cruelty:
Yet you, the murderer, look as bright, as clear,
As yonder Venus in her glimmering sphere.
HERMIA. What's this to my Lysander? where is he?
Ah, good Demetrius, wilt thou give him me?
DEMETRIUS. I had rather give his carcass to my hounds.
HERMIA. Out, dog! out, cur! thou driv'st me past the bounds
Of maiden's patience. Hast thou slain him, then?
Henceforth be never number'd among men!
Oh! once tell true; tell true, even for my sake;
Durst thou have look'd upon him, being awake,
And hast thou kill'd him sleeping? O brave touch!^{25}
Could not a worm, an adder, do so much?
An adder did it; for with doubler tongue
Than thine, thou serpent, never adder stung.
DEMETRIUS. You spend your passion on a mispris'd mood:^{26}
I am not guilty of Lysander's blood;
Nor is he dead, for aught that I can tell.
HERMIA. I pray thee, tell me, then, that he is well.
DEMETRIUS. An if I could, what should I get therefore?
HERMIA. A privilege never to see me more.—
And from thy hated presence part I so:
See me no more whether he be dead or no. [*Exit.*]
DEMETRIUS. There is no following her in this fierce vein:
Here, therefore, for a while I will remain.
So sorrow's heaviness doth heavier grow
For debt that bankrupt sleep doth sorrow owe;
Which now in some slight measure it will pay,
If for his tender here I make some stay.

---

^{25} A *touch* anciently signified a *trick* or *feat*. Ascham has "The shrewd *touches* of many curst boys." And, in the old story of *Howleglas*, "For at all times he did some mad *touch*."

^{26} "On a misprised mood" probably means *in a mistaken manner*. *On* and *in* were sometimes used interchangeably; as also *mood* and *mode* appear to have been. To *misprise* is to *prise amiss*, or to *misapprehend*.

[*Lies down and sleeps.*]

OBERON. What hast thou done? thou hast mistaken quite,
And laid the love-juice on some true-love's sight:
Of thy misprision must perforce ensue
Some true love turn'd, and not a false turn'd true.
PUCK. Then fate o'er-rules, that, one man holding troth,
A million fail, confounding oath on oath.
OBERON. About the wood go, swifter than the wind,
And Helena of Athens look thou find:
All fancy-sick she is, and pale of cheer[27]
With sighs of love, that costs the fresh blood dear:[28]
By some illusion see thou bring her here;
I'll charm his eyes against she do appear.
PUCK. I go, I go; look how I go,—
Swifter than arrow from the Tartar's bow. [*Exit.*]
OBERON.   Flower of this purple dye,
Hit with Cupid's archery,
Sink in apple of his eye!

[*Squeezing the juice on* DEMETRIUS'*s eyelids.*]

When his love he doth espy,
Let her shine as gloriously
As the Venus of the sky.—
When thou wak'st, if she be by,
Beg of her for remedy.

[*Re-enter* PUCK.]

PUCK. Captain of our fairy band,
Helena is here at hand,
And the youth mistook by me
Pleading for a lover's fee;
Shall we their fond pageant see?
Lord, what fools these mortals be!
OBERON. Stand aside: the noise they make
Will cause Demetrius to awake.

---

[27] *Cheer* is from the old French *chire,* which Cotgrave thus explains: "The face, visage, countenance, favour, looks, aspect." Hence it naturally came to mean that which *affects* the face, or gives it expression.—Here, again, *fancy-sick* is *love-sick.* See page 18, note 13.

[28] According to the old notion, that every sigh consumed a drop of blood. So Shakespeare has the phrases, "blood-*consuming* sighs," "blood-*drinking* sighs," and blood-*sucking* sighs."

PUCK. Then will two at once woo one,—
    That must needs be sport alone;[29]
    And those things do best please me
    That befall preposterously.

    [*Re-enter* LYSANDER *and* HELENA.]

LYSANDER. Why should you think that I should[30] woo in scorn?
    Scorn and derision never come in tears.
    Look when I vow, I weep; and vows so born,
    In their nativity all truth appears.
    How can these things in me seem scorn to you,
    Bearing the badge of faith, to prove them true?
HELENA. You do advance your cunning more and more.
    When truth kills truth, O devilish-holy fray!
    These vows are Hermia's: will you give her o'er?
    Weigh oath with oath, and you will nothing weigh:
    Your vows to her and me, put in two scales,
    Will even weigh; and both as light as tales.
LYSANDER. I had no judgment when to her I swore.
HELENA. Nor none, in my mind, now you give her o'er.
LYSANDER. Demetrius loves her, and he loves not you.
DEMETRIUS [*Awaking.*] O Helen, goddess, nymph, perfect, divine!
    To what, my love, shall I compare thine eyne?
    Crystal is muddy. O, how ripe in show
    Thy lips, those kissing cherries, tempting grow!
    That pure congealed white, high Taurus' snow,
    Fann'd with the eastern wind, turns to a crow
    When thou hold'st up thy hand: O, let me kiss
    This princess of pure white, this seal of bliss![31]
HELENA. O spite! O hell! I see you all are bent
    To set against me for your merriment.
    If you were civil, and knew courtesy,
    You would not do me thus much injury.

---

    [29] *Rare* sport; sport so good as to spoil all other.
    [30] *Should* where present usage requires *would.* The auxiliaries *could, should,* and *would* were often used indiscriminately.
    [31] So in *Antony and Cleopatra,* iii. 13: "My playfellow, your hand; this kingly *seal,* and plighter of high hearts." *Princess* here plainly has the force of the surperlative; the *paragon,* the *purest* of white.—This pretty piece of extravagance reminds me of Spenser's Una:

        A lovely ladie rode him faire beside,
        Upon a lowly ass more white than snow;
        Yet she much whiter.

Can you not hate me, as I know you do,
But you must join in souls[32] to mock me too?
If you were men, as men you are in show,
You would not use a gentle lady so;
To vow, and swear, and superpraise my parts,
When I am sure you hate me with your hearts.
You both are rivals, and love Hermia;
And now both rivals, to mock Helena:
A trim exploit, a manly enterprise,
To conjure tears up in a poor maid's eyes
With your derision! None of noble sort[33]
Would so offend a virgin, and extort
A poor soul's patience, all to make you sport.
LYSANDER. You are unkind, Demetrius; be not so;
For you love Hermia: this you know I know:
And here, with all good will, with all my heart,
In Hermia's love I yield you up my part;
And yours of Helena to me bequeath,
Whom I do love and will do till my death.
HELENA. Never did mockers waste more idle breath.
DEMETRIUS. Lysander, keep thy Hermia; I will none:
If e'er I lov'd her, all that love is gone.
My heart to her but as guest-wise sojourn'd;
And now to Helen is it home return'd,
There to remain.
LYSANDER. Helen, it is not so.
DEMETRIUS. Disparage not the faith thou dost not know,
Lest, to thy peril, thou aby[34] it dear.—
Look where thy love comes; yonder is thy dear.

[*Re-enter* HERMIA.]

HERMIA. Dark night, that from the eye his function takes,
The ear more quick of apprehension makes;
Wherein it doth impair the seeing sense,
It pays the hearing double recompense:—
Thou art not by mine eye, Lysander, found;

---

[32] That is, join *heartily*, or *in earnest*; be *of the same mind.*
[33] *Sort* here means *rank* or *quality*; a common use of the word in Shakespeare's time. So in *Henry V.*, iv. 7: "It may be his enemy is a gentleman of great *sort.*"
[34] *Aby* or *abie* means to *suffer for.* Skinner thinks it is formed, not from *abide* but from *buy*; though the two are often confounded. So in *The Faerie Queene*, ii. 8, 33: "That direfull stroke thou dearely shalt *aby.*" And in Beaumont and Fletcher's *Knight of the Burning Pestle*: "Foolhardy knight, full soon thou shalt *aby* this fond reproach; thy body will I bang."

Mine ear, I thank it, brought me to thy sound.
But why unkindly didst thou leave me so?
LYSANDER. Why should he stay whom love doth press to go?
HERMIA. What love could press Lysander from my side?
LYSANDER. Lysander's love, that would not let him bide,—
Fair Helena,—who more engilds the night
Than all yon fiery oes and eyes of light.
Why seek'st thou me? could not this make thee know
The hate I bare thee made me leave thee so?
HERMIA. You speak not as you think; it cannot be.
HELENA. Lo, she is one of this confederacy!
Now I perceive they have conjoin'd all three
To fashion this false sport in spite of me.
Injurious Hermia! most ungrateful maid!
Have you conspir'd, have you with these contriv'd,
To bait[35] me with this foul derision?
Is all the counsel that we two have shar'd,
The sisters' vows, the hours that we have spent,
When we have chid the hasty-footed time
For parting us,—O, is all forgot?
All school-days' friendship, childhood innocence?
We, Hermia, like two artificial[36] gods,
Have with our needls[37] created both one flower,
Both on one sampler, sitting on one cushion,
Both warbling of one song, both in one key;
As if our hands, our sides, voices, and minds,
Had been incorporate.[38] So we grew together,
Like to a double cherry, seeming parted;
But yet a union in partition,
Two lovely berries moulded on one stem:
So, with two seeming bodies, but one heart;
Two of the first, like coats in heraldry,
Due but to one, and crowned with one crest.[39]

---

[35] To *bait* is to *worry*, to *bark at*, as bears used to be baited by dogs in the old bear-baiting times. So in *The Faerie Queene*, ii. 8, 42: "A salvage bull, whom two fierce mastives *bayt*."

[36] *Artificial* is here used for the *worker* in art, not the *work*; like its Latin original *artifex*, artist, or artificer.

[37] *Neeld* was a common contraction of *needle*.

[38] Gibbon, in his account of the friendship between the great Cappadocian saints, Basil and Gregory Nazianzen, *Decline and Fall*, chap, xxvii., note 29, refers to this passage, and quotes a parallel passage from Gregory's Poem on his own Life. The historian adds, "Shakespeare had never read the poems of Gregory Nazianzen, he was ignorant of the Greek language; but his mother-tongue, the language of Nature, is the same in Cappadocia and in Britain."

And will you rent our ancient love asunder,
To join with men in scorning your poor friend?
It is not friendly, 'tis not maidenly:
Our sex, as well as I, may chide you for it,
Though I alone do feel the injury.
HERMIA. I am amazed at your passionate words:
I scorn you not; it seems that you scorn me.
HELENA. Have you not set Lysander, as in scorn,
To follow me, and praise my eyes and face?
And made your other love, Demetrius,—
Who even but now did spurn me with his foot,—
To call me goddess, nymph, divine, and rare,
Precious, celestial? Wherefore speaks he this
To her he hates? and wherefore doth Lysander
Deny your love, so rich within his soul,
And tender me, forsooth, affection,
But by your setting on, by your consent?
What though I be not so in grace as you,
So hung upon with love, so fortunate;
But miserable most, to love unlov'd?
This you should pity rather than despise.
HERMIA. I understand not what you mean by this.
HELENA. Ay, do persever, counterfeit sad looks,
Make mows upon me when I turn my back;
Wink each at other; hold the sweet jest up:
This sport, well carried, shall be chronicled.
If you have any pity, grace, or manners,
You would not make me such an argument.[40]
But fare ye well: 'tis partly my own fault;
Which death, or absence, soon shall remedy.
LYSANDER. Stay, gentle Helena; hear my excuse;
My love, my life, my soul, fair Helena!
HELENA. O excellent!
HERMIA. Sweet, do not scorn her so.
DEMETRIUS. If she cannot entreat, I can compel.
LYSANDER. Thou canst compel no more than she entreat;
Thy threats have no more strength than her weak prayers.—
Helen, I love thee; by my life I do;
I swear by that which I will lose for thee
To prove him false that says I love thee not.

---

[39] Douce thus explains this passage: "We had *two of the first*, i.e., *bodies*, like the double coats in heraldry that belong to man and wife as *one person*, but which, like our *single heart*, have but *one crest*."

[40] *Argument*, here, is *subject* or *theme of sport*.

DEMETRIUS. I say I love thee more than he can do.
LYSANDER. If thou say so, withdraw, and prove it too.
DEMETRIUS. Quick, come,—
HERMIA. Lysander, whereto tends all this?
LYSANDER. Away, you Ethiop!
DEMETRIUS. No, no, sir:—he will
    Seem to break loose; take on as you would follow:
    But yet come not. You are a tame man; go!
LYSANDER. Hang off, thou cat, thou burr: vile thing, let loose,
    Or I will shake thee from me like a serpent.
HERMIA. Why are you grown so rude? what change is this,
    Sweet love?
LYSANDER. Thy love! out, tawny Tartar, out!
    Out, loathed medicine! hated potion, hence!
HERMIA. Do you not jest?
HELENA. Yes, sooth;[41] and so do you.
LYSANDER. Demetrius, I will keep my word with thee.
DEMETRIUS. I would I had your bond; for I perceive
    A weak bond holds you; I'll not trust your word.
LYSANDER. What! should I hurt her, strike her, kill her dead?
    Although I hate her, I'll not harm her so.
HERMIA. What! can you do me greater harm than hate?
    Hate me! wherefore? O me! what news, my love?
    Am not I Hermia? Are not you Lysander?
    I am as fair now as I was erewhile.
    Since night you lov'd me; yet since night you left me:
    Why then, you left me,—O, the gods forbid!—
    In earnest, shall I say?
LYSANDER. Ay, by my life;
    And never did desire to see thee more.
    Therefore be out of hope, of question, doubt,
    Be certain, nothing truer; 'tis no jest
    That I do hate thee and love Helena.
HERMIA. O me! you juggler! you canker-blossom![42]
    You thief of love! What! have you come by night,
    And stol'n my love's heart from him?
HELENA. Fine, i' faith!
    Have you no modesty, no maiden shame,
    No touch of bashfulness? What! will you tear

---

[41] *Sooth* is *truth*; as in *soothsayer*, which originally meant *truth-speaker*.

[42] The *canker* is a worm that preys on the leaves or buds of flowers, always beginning in the middle. So before, in this play: "Some to kill *cankers* in the musk-rose buds."—The verse requires *juggler* here to be a trisyllable. It appears that divers similar words were sometimes so pronounced.

Impatient answers from my gentle tongue?
Fie, fie! you counterfeit, you puppet, you!
HERMIA. Puppet! why so? Ay, that way goes the game.
Now I perceive that she hath made compare
Between our statures; she hath urg'd her height;
And with her personage, her tall personage,
Her height, forsooth, she hath prevail'd with him.—
And are you grown so high in his esteem
Because I am so dwarfish and so low?
How low am I, thou painted maypole? speak;
How low am I? I am not yet so low
But that my nails can reach unto thine eyes.
HELENA. I pray you, though you mock me, gentlemen,
Let her not hurt me. I was never curst;[43]
I have no gift at all in shrewishness;
I am a right maid for my cowardice;
Let her not strike me. You perhaps may think,
Because she is something lower than myself,
That I can match her.
HERMIA. Lower! hark, again.
HELENA. Good Hermia, do not be so bitter with me.
I evermore did love you, Hermia;
Did ever keep your counsels; never wrong'd you;
Save that, in love unto Demetrius,
I told him of your stealth unto this wood:
He follow'd you; for love I follow'd him;
But he hath chid me hence, and threaten'd me
To strike me, spurn me, nay, to kill me too:
And now, so you will let me quiet go,
To Athens will I bear my folly back,
And follow you no farther. Let me go:
You see how simple and how fond I am.
HERMIA. Why, get you gone: who is't that hinders you?
HELENA. A foolish heart that I leave here behind.
HERMIA. What! with Lysander?
HELENA. With Demetrius.
LYSANDER. Be not afraid; she shall not harm thee, Helena.
DEMETRIUS. No, sir, she shall not, though you take her part.
HELENA. O, when she's angry, she is keen and shrewd:
She was a vixen when she went to school;
And, though she be but little, she is fierce.
HERMIA. Little again! nothing but low and little!—

---

[43] *Curst* is *shrewish, spiteful, scolding;* often so used.

Why will you suffer her to flout me thus?
Let me come to her.
LYSANDER. Get you gone, you dwarf;
You minimus, of hind'ring knot-grass[44] made;
You bead, you acorn.
DEMETRIUS. You are too officious
In her behalf that scorns your services.
Let her alone: speak not of Helena;
Take not her part; for if thou dost intend[45]
Never so little show of love to her,
Thou shalt aby it.[46]
LYSANDER. Now she holds me not;
Now follow, if thou dar'st, to try whose right,
Of thine or mine,[47] is most in Helena.
DEMETRIUS. Follow! nay, I'll go with thee, cheek by jowl.[48]

[*Exeunt* LYSANDER *and* DEMETRIUS.]

HERMIA. You, mistress, all this coil is 'long[49] of you:
Nay, go not back.
HELENA. I will not trust you, I;
Nor longer stay in your curst company.
Your hands than mine are quicker for a fray;
My legs are longer though, to run away. [*Exit.*]
HERMIA. I am amaz'd, and know not what to say. [*Exit.*]
OBERON. This is thy negligence: still thou mistak'st,
Or else commit'st thy knaveries willfully.
PUCK. Believe me, king of shadows, I mistook.
Did not you tell me I should know the man
By the Athenian garments he had on?
And so far blameless proves my enterprise
That I have 'nointed an Athenian's eyes:
And so far am I glad it so did sort,[50]

---

[44] *Knot-grass*, it seems, was anciently supposed to stop the growth of those to whom it was applied. So in Beaumont and Fletcher's *Knight of the Burning Pestle*, ii. 2: "The child's a fatherless child, and say they should put him into a strait pair of gaskins, 'twere worse than *knot-grass*; he would *never grow* after it."

[45] *Intend* with the sense of *pretend*; the Poet has it repeatedly so. In fact, the two words were used interchangeably, and we often have either in the sense of the other.

[46] *Suffer* or *pay dearly for* it; *rue* it. See page 54, note 34.

[47] This is in accordance with old usage. We have another instance in *The Tempest*, ii. 1: "Which, *of he or Adrian*, for a good wager, first begins to crow?"

[48] That is, *side by side*, or *with cheeks close together. Jowl* is, properly, *jaw*, or *jaw-bone.*

[49] *Along of\s* an old phrase exactly equivalent to *because of*, so used by all writers in Shakespeare's time, and occasionally used still.—*Coil* is *stir, bustle, turmoil.*

As this their jangling I esteem a sport.

OBERON. Thou seest these lovers seek a place to fight;
Hie therefore, Robin, overcast the night;
The starry welkin cover thou anon
With drooping fog, as black as Acheron,
And lead these testy rivals so astray
As one come not within another's way.
Like to Lysander sometime[51] frame thy tongue,
Then stir Demetrius up with bitter wrong;
And sometime rail thou like Demetrius;
And from each other look thou lead them thus,
Till o'er their brows death-counterfeiting sleep
With leaden legs and batty wings doth creep:
Then crush this herb into Lysander's eye;
Whose liquor hath this virtuous property,
To take from thence all error with his[52] might
And make his eyeballs roll with wonted sight.
When they next wake, all this derision
Shall seem a dream and fruitless vision;
And back to Athens shall the lovers wend
With league whose date till death shall never end.
Whiles I in this affair do thee employ,
I'll to my queen, and beg her Indian boy;
And then I will her charmed eye release
From monster's view, and all things shall be peace.

PUCK. My fairy lord, this must be done with haste,
For night's swift dragons[53] cut the clouds full fast;
And yonder shines Aurora's harbinger,
At whose approach ghosts, wandering here and there,
Troop home to churchyards: damned spirits all,
That in cross-ways and floods have burial,[54]

---

[50] *Sort*, here, is *fall out, happen*, or *come to pass*. So in *Much Ado*, v. 4: "I am glad that all things *sort* so well." The usage was common.

[51] *Sometime* for *sometimes*. See page 29, note 7.

[52] *His* for *its*, referring to *liquor*; *its* not being then an accepted word.

[53] The chariot of Madam Night was anciently drawn by a team of dragons, that is, serpents, who were thought to be always awake, because they slept with their eyes open; and therefore were selected for this purpose. So in *Cymbeline*, ii. 2: "Swift, swift, ye *dragons* of the night." And in Milton's *Il Penseroso*:

> Smoothing the rugged brow of night,
> While Cynthia checks her *dragon* yoke.

[54] The ghosts of self-murderers, who were buried in crossroads; and of those who being drowned were condemned (according to the opinion of the ancients) to wander for a hundred years, as the rites of sepulture had never been regularly bestowed on their

Already to their wormy beds are gone;
For fear lest day should look their shames upon
They wilfully exile themselves from light,
And must for aye consort with black-brow'd night.
OBERON. But we are spirits of another sort:
I with the morning's love[55] have oft made sport;
And, like a forester, the groves may tread
Even till the eastern gate, all fiery-red,
Opening on Neptune with fair blessed beams,
Turns into yellow gold his salt-green streams.
But, notwithstanding, haste; make no delay:
We may effect this business yet ere day. [*Exit.*]
PUCK. Up and down, up and down;
I will lead them up and down:
I am fear'd in field and town.
Goblin, lead them up and down.
Here comes one.

[*Enter* LYSANDER.]

LYSANDER. Where art thou, proud Demetrius? speak thou now.
PUCK. Here, villain; drawn and ready. Where art thou?
LYSANDER. I will be with thee straight.
PUCK. Follow me, then,
To plainer ground. [*Exit* LYSANDER *as following the voice.*]

[*Enter* DEMETRIUS.]

DEMETRIUS. Lysander! speak again.
Thou runaway, thou coward, art thou fled?
Speak. In some bush? where dost thou hide thy head?
PUCK. Thou coward, art thou bragging to the stars,
Telling the bushes that thou look'st for wars,
And wilt not come? Come, recreant; come, thou child;
I'll whip thee with a rod: he is defiled
That draws a sword on thee.
DEMETRIUS. Yea, art thou there?
PUCK. Follow my voice; we'll try no manhood here.

---

bodies. See the passage in *Hamlet*, act i., sc. I: "I have heard, the cock that is the trumpet to the morn," &c.

[55] The allusion is, probably, to Cephalus, who was a mighty hunter. Aurora became enamoured of him, and took him for her *love*. So in *The Phœnix Nest*, 1593: "Aurora now began to rise againe from watrie couch and from old Tithon's side, in hope to *kisse* upon Acteian plaine yong *Cephalus.*"

[*Exeunt.*]

[*Re-enter* LYSANDER.]

LYSANDER. He goes before me, and still dares me on;
    When I come where he calls, then he is gone.
    The villain is much lighter heeled than I:
    I follow'd fast, but faster he did fly;
    That fallen am I in dark uneven way,
    And here will rest me. [*Lies down.*]—Come, thou gentle day!
    For if but once thou show me thy grey light,
    I'll find Demetrius, and revenge this spite. [*Sleeps.*]

[*Re-enter* PUCK *and* DEMETRIUS.]

PUCK. Ho, ho, ho, ho![56] Coward, why com'st thou not?
DEMETRIUS. Abide me, if thou dar'st; for well I wot
    Thou runn'st before me, shifting every place;
    And dar'st not stand, nor look me in the face.
    Where art thou?
PUCK. Come hither; I am here.
DEMETRIUS. Nay, then, thou mock'st me. Thou shalt 'by[57] this dear,
    If ever I thy face by daylight see:
    Now, go thy way. Faintness constraineth me
    To measure out my length on this cold bed.—
    By day's approach look to be visited. [*Lies down and sleeps.*]

[*Re-enter* HELENA.]

HELENA. O weary night, O long and tedious night,
    Abate thy hours! Shine comforts from the east,
    That I may back to Athens by daylight,
    From these that my poor company detest:—
    And sleep, that sometimes shuts up sorrow's eye,
    Steal me awhile from mine own company. [*Lies down and sleeps.*]
PUCK. Yet but three? Come one more;
    Two of both kinds makes up four.

---

[56] A strong dash of malignant, or mischievous sportiveness belongs to this character. There was an old local proverb, "To laugh like Robin Goodfellow"; which probably meant, to laugh in mockery or scorn. In the old Moral-plays, as also in the older Miracle-plays, the Devil was generally one of the leading characters, and his laughter of fiendish mirth was always expressed as in the text. So in *Gammer Gurton's Needle*: "But, Diccon, Diccon, did not the Devil cry *ho, ho, ho?*"

[57] '*By* for *aby*, as before explained; page 59, note 46.

Here she comes, curst and sad:—
Cupid is a knavish lad,
Thus to make poor females mad.

[*Re-enter* HERMIA.]

HERMIA. Never so weary, never so in woe,
Bedabbled with the dew, and torn with briers;
I can no further crawl, no further go;
My legs can keep no pace with my desires.
Here will I rest me till the break of day.
Heavens shield Lysander, if they mean a fray!

[*Lies down and sleeps.*]

PUCK. On the ground sleep sound:
I'll apply to your eye,
Gentle lover, remedy.
[*Squeezing the herb on* LYSANDER's *eyelids.*]
When thou wak'st, thou tak'st
True delight in the sight
Of thy former lady's eye:
And the country proverb known,
That every man should take his own,
In your waking shall be shown:
Jack shall have Jill;[58]
Nought shall go ill;
The man shall have his mare again, and all shall be well. [*Exit.*]

---

[58] This proverb is quoted repeatedly in old plays; and its meaning is much the same as that of the other proverbial sayings here clustered with it. So in *Love's Labours Lost*, v. 2: "Our wooing doth not end like an old play; *Jack hath not Jill.*" And in Heywood, 1598: "Come chat at home, *all is* well, Jack shall have Jill."

ACT IV.

SCENE I.

The Wood. LYSANDER, DEMETRIUS, HELENA,
and HERMIA, *lying asleep.*

[*Enter* TITANIA *and* BOTTOM; PEAS-BLOSSOM, COBWEB,
MOTH, MUSTARDSEED, *and other* FAIRIES *attending*;
OBERON *behind, unseen.*]

TITANIA. Come, sit thee down upon this flowery bed,
    While I thy amiable cheeks do coy,[1]
    And stick musk-roses in thy sleek smooth head,
    And kiss thy fair large ears, my gentle joy.
BOTTOM. Where's Peas-blossom?
PEAS-BLOSSOM. Ready.
BOTTOM. Scratch my head, Peas-blossom.—
    Where's Monsieur Cobweb?
COBWEB. Ready.
BOTTOM. Monsieur Cobweb; good monsieur, get you your weapons
    in your hand and kill me a red-hipped humble-bee on the top of a
    thistle; and, good monsieur, bring me the honey-bag. Do not fret
    yourself too much in the action, monsieur; and, good monsieur,
    have a care the honey-bag break not; I would be loath to have you
    overflown with a honey-bag, signior.—Where's Monsieur
    Mustardseed?
MUSTARDSEED. Ready.
BOTTOM. Give me your neif,[2] Monsieur Mustardseed. Pray you, leave
    your curtsy, good monsieur.
MUSTARDSEED. What's your will?
BOTTOM. Nothing, good monsieur, but to help Cavalery Cobweb[3] to
    scratch. I must to the barber's, monsieur; for methinks I am
    marvellous hairy about the face; and I am such a tender ass, if my
    hair do but tickle me I must scratch.
TITANIA. What, wilt thou hear some music, my sweet love?
BOTTOM. I have a reasonable good ear in music; let us have the tongs
    and the bones. [*Rough music.*]

---

[1] To *coy* is to *stroke* with the hand, to *fondle*, or *caress.*

[2] *Neif* is an old word for *fist.* So in *2 Henry IV.*, ii. 4: "Sweet knight, I kiss thy *neif.*"

[3] Bottom is here in a strange predicament, and has not had time to perfect himself in
the nomenclature of his fairy attendants; and so he gets the names somewhat mixed.
Probably he is here addressing Cavalery Peasblossom, but gives him the wrong name.

TITANIA. Or say, sweet love, what thou desirest to eat.
BOTTOM. Truly, a peck of provender; I could munch your good dry
   oats. Methinks I have a great desire to a bottle[4] of hay: good hay,
   sweet hay, hath no fellow.
TITANIA. I have a venturous fairy that shall seek
   The squirrel's hoard, and fetch thee new nuts.
BOTTOM. I had rather have a handful or two of dried peas. But, I pray
   you, let none of your people stir me; I have an exposition of sleep
   come upon me.
TITANIA. Fairies, be gone, and be all ways away.—

[*Exeunt* FAIRIES.]

Sleep thou, and I will wind thee in my arms.
So doth the woodbine the sweet honeysuckle
Gently entwist,[5] the female ivy so
Enrings the barky fingers of the elm.
O, how I love thee! how I dote on thee! [*They sleep.*]

[*Enter* PUCK.]

OBERON [*Advancing.*] Welcome, good Robin. Seest thou this sweet
sight?
   Her dotage now I do begin to pity.
   For, meeting her of late behind the wood,
   Seeking sweet favours[6] for this hateful fool,
   I did upbraid her and fall out with her:
   For she his hairy temples then had rounded
   With coronet of fresh and fragrant flowers;
   And that same dew, which sometime on the buds
   Was wont to swell like round and orient pearls,
   Stood now within the pretty flow'rets' eyes,
   Like tears that did their own disgrace bewail.
   When I had, at my pleasure, taunted her,

---

   [4] *Bottle* is an old word for *bundle*, from the French *boteau*. Richardson says, "It is
still common in the northern parts of England to call a truss or bundle of hay *a bottle*."

   [5] Odd work has sometimes been made with this passage by explaining *woodbine*
and *honeysuckle* as meaning the same thing; and Singer's explanation still proceeds upon
an identity of the two plants. In Jonson's *Vision of Delight* we have the following:
"Behold, how the blue *bindweed* doth itself infold with *honeysuckle*?" Upon this passage
Gifford notes as follows: "The woodbine of Shakespeare is the blue bindweed of Jonson:
in many of our counties woodbine is still the name for the great convolvulus."

   [6] So in Greene's *Quip for an Upstart Courtier*, quoted by Dyce: "These with syren-
like allurement so entised these quaint squires, that they bestowed all their *flowers* upon
them for *favours.*"

And she, in mild terms, begg'd my patience,
I then did ask of her her changeling child;
Which straight she gave me, and her fairy sent
To bear him to my bower in fairy-land.
And now I have the boy, I will undo
This hateful imperfection of her eyes.
And, gentle Puck, take this transformed scalp
From off the head of this Athenian swain,
That he awaking when the other do,
May all to Athens back again repair,
And think no more of this night's accidents
But as the fierce vexation of a dream.
But first I will release the fairy queen.
 Be as thou wast wont to be;

[*Touching her eyes with an herb.*]

 See as thou was wont to see.
 Dian's bud[7] o'er Cupid's flower
 Hath such force and blessed power.
Now, my Titania; wake you, my sweet queen.
TITANIA. My Oberon! what visions have I seen!
 Methought I was enamour'd of an ass.
OBERON. There lies your love.
TITANIA. How came these things to pass?
 O, how mine eyes do loathe his visage now!
OBERON. Silence awhile.—Robin, take off this head.
 Titania, music call; and strike more dead
 Than common sleep, of all these five, the sense.
TITANIA. Music, ho! music; such as charmeth sleep.
PUCK. Now when thou wak'st, with thine own fool's eyes peep.
OBERON. Sound, music. [*Still music.*]—Come, my queen, take hands
with me,

And rock the ground whereon these sleepers be.
Now thou and I are new in amity,
And will to-morrow midnight solemnly
Dance in Duke Theseus' house triumphantly,
And bless it to all fair prosperity:
There shall the pairs of faithful lovers be
Wedded, with Theseus, all in jollity.

---

[7] *Dian's Bud* is the bud of the *Agnus Castus*, or *Chaste Tree*. "The vertue of this
hearbe is, that he will kepe man and woman *chaste*." Macer's *Herbal*, by Lynacre.
Cupid's flower is the *Viola tricolour*, or *Love-in-Idleness*.

PUCK.   Fairy king, attend and mark;
             I do hear the morning lark.
OBERON.   Then, my queen, in silence sad,[8]
             Trip we after night's shade.
             We the globe can compass soon,
             Swifter than the wand'ring moon.
TITANIA.   Come, my lord; and in our flight,
             Tell me how it came this night
             That I sleeping here was found
             With these mortals on the ground. [*Exeunt.*]

       [*Horns sound within.*]

       [*Enter* THESEUS, HIPPOLYTA, EGEUS, *and Train.*]

THESEUS. Go, one of you, find out the forester;—
       For now our observation[9] is perform'd;
       And since we have the vaward[10] of the day,
       My love shall hear the music of my hounds,—
       Uncouple in the western valley; go:—
       Despatch, I say, and find the forester.—[*Exit an* ATTENDANT.]
       We will, fair queen, up to the mountain's top,
       And mark the musical confusion
       Of hounds and echo in conjunction.
HIPPOLYTA. I was with Hercules and Cadmus once
       When in a wood of Crete they bay'd the bear
       With hounds of Sparta: never did I hear
       Such gallant chiding;[11] for, besides the groves,
       The skies, the fountains, every region near
       Seem'd all one mutual cry: I never heard
       So musical a discord, such sweet thunder.
THESEUS. My hounds are bred out of the Spartan kind,
       So flew'd, so sanded;[12] and their heads are hung
       With ears that sweep away the morning dew;
       Crook-knee'd and dew-lap'd like Thessalian bulls;

---

[8] *Sad* here signifies only *grave, serious.* Often so.
[9] The honours due to the morning of *May.* So in a former scene: "To do *observance* to a morn of May."
[10] The early part, the *vanward,* of the day.
[11] *Chiding* means here the *cry of hounds.* To *chide* is used sometimes for to *sound,* or *make a noise,* without any reference to scolding. So in *Henry VIII.*: "As doth a rock against the *chiding* flood."
[12] The *flews* are the large chops of a deep-mouthed hound.—*Sanded* means of *a sandy colour,* which is one of the true denotements of a bloodhound.

Slow in pursuit, but match'd in mouth like bells,
Each under each.[13] A cry more tuneable
Was never holla'd to, nor cheer'd with horn,
In Crete, in Sparta, nor in Thessaly.
Judge when you hear.—But, soft, what nymphs are these?
EGEUS. My lord, this is my daughter here asleep;
And this Lysander; this Demetrius is;
This Helena, old Nedar's Helena:
I wonder of their being here together.
THESEUS. No doubt they rose up early to observe
The rite of May; and, hearing our intent,
Came here in grace of our solemnity.—
But speak, Egeus; is not this the day
That Hermia should give answer of her choice?
EGEUS. It is, my lord.
THESEUS. Go, bid the huntsmen wake them with their horns.

[*Exit an* ATTENDANT. *Horns and shouts within.* LYSANDER,
DEMETRIUS, HELENA, *and* HERMIA, *awake and start up.*]

Good-morrow, friends. Saint Valentine is past;
Begin these wood-birds but to couple now?
LYSANDER. Pardon, my lord. [*He and the rest kneel to* THESEUS.]
THESEUS. I pray you all, stand up.
I know you two are rival enemies;
How comes this gentle concord in the world,
That hatred is so far from jealousy
To sleep by hate, and fear no enmity?
LYSANDER. My lord, I shall reply amazedly,
Half sleep, half waking; but as yet, I swear,
I cannot truly say how I came here:
But, as I think,—for truly would I speak—
And now I do bethink me, so it is,—
I came with Hermia hither: our intent
Was to be gone from Athens, where we might be,
Without[14] the peril of the Athenian law.

---

[13] "Match'd in mouth like bells" is with their several barking-tones so pitched as to harmonize with each other, like a chime of bells. This is shown by *The Edinburgh Review* for October, 1872. "It was a ruling consideration," says the writer, "in the formation of a pack, that it should possess the musical fulness and strength of a perfect canine quire. And hounds of good voice were selected and arranged in the hunting chorus on the same general principles that govern the formation of a cathedral or any other more articulate choir." And this is fully justified by extracts from a writer contemporary with the Poet; which, however, are too long for quotation here.

[14] *Without* is here equivalent to *beyond*. The Poet has it repeatedly so.

EGEUS. Enough, enough, my lord; you have enough;
    I beg the law, the law upon his head.—
    They would have stol'n away, they would, Demetrius,
    Thereby to have defeated you and me:
    You of your wife, and me of my consent,—
    Of my consent that she should be your wife.
DEMETRIUS. My lord, fair Helen told me of their stealth,
    Of this their purpose hither to this wood;
    And I in fury hither follow'd them,
    Fair Helena in fancy following me.
    But, my good lord, I wot not by what power,—
    But by some power it is,—my love to Hermia,
    Melted as the snow—seems to me now
    As the remembrance of an idle gaud
    Which in my childhood I did dote upon:
    And all the faith, the virtue of my heart,
    The object and the pleasure of mine eye,
    Is only Helena. To her, my lord,
    Was I betroth'd ere I saw Hermia:
    But, like[15] a sickness, did I loathe this food;
    But, as in health, come to my natural taste,
    Now I do wish it, love it, long for it,
    And will for evermore be true to it.
THESEUS. Fair lovers, you are fortunately met:
    Of this discourse we more will hear anon.—
    Egeus, I will overbear your will;
    For in the temple, by and by with us,
    These couples shall eternally be knit.
    And, for[16] the morning now is something worn,
    Our purpos'd hunting shall be set aside.—
    Away with us to Athens, three and three,
    We'll hold a feast in great solemnity.—
    Come, Hippolyta.

[*Exeunt* THESEUS, HIPPOLYTA, EGEUS, *and Train.*]

DEMETRIUS. These things seem small and undistinguishable,
    Like far-off mountains turned into clouds.
HERMIA. Methinks I see these things with parted eye,[17]

---

    [15] *Like* was sometimes used with the force of the conjunction *as.* The usage still holds in some parts of the United States.

    [16] Here, as often, *for* is equivalent to *because, inasmuch as,* or *since.*

    [17] "With *parted* eye" means, apparently, with the *two eyes* acting *separately* or independently, and not together or *as one.*

When every thing seems double.
HELENA. So methinks:
And I have found Demetrius like a jewel.
Mine own, and not mine own.[18]
DEMETRIUS. It seems to me
That yet we sleep, we dream.—Do not you think
The duke was here, and bid us follow him?
HERMIA. Yea, and my father.
HELENA. And Hippolyta.
LYSANDER. And he did bid us follow to the temple.
DEMETRIUS. Why, then, we are awake: let's follow him;
And by the way let us recount our dreams. [*Exeunt.*]
BOTTOM. [*Awaking.*] When my cue comes, call me, and I will
answer. My next is *Most fair Pyramus.*—Heigh-ho!—Peter
Quince! Flute, the bellows-mender! Snout, the tinker! Starveling!
God's my life, stol'n hence, and left me asleep! I have had a most
rare vision. I have had a dream—past the wit of man to say what
dream it was.—Man is but an ass if he go about to expound this
dream. Methought I was—there is no man can tell what.
Methought I was, and methought I had,—but man is but a patch'd
fool,[19] if he will offer to say what methought I had. The eye of man
hath not heard, the ear of man hath not seen; man's hand is not
able to taste, his tongue to conceive, nor his heart to report, what
my dream was. I will get Peter Quince to write a ballad of this
dream: it shall be called *Bottom's Dream*, because it hath no
bottom; and I will sing it in the latter end of a play, before the
duke: peradventure, to make it the more gracious, I shall sing it at
her death.[20] [*Exit.*]

---

[18] "As the jewel which one finds is his own and not his own; his own, unless the
loser claims it." Not a very satisfactory explanation, perhaps; but the best that is
forthcoming. How Demetrius has been Helen's own and not her own, and thus like a
double man, is plain enough; but the simile of the jewel is not so clear.

[19] I have several times noted the Poet's frequent use of *patch* for *fool.* In illustration
of the matter, Staunton tells of his having seen a Flemish picture of the sixteenth
century," which represents a procession of masquers and mummers, led by a Fool or
jester, whose dress is covered with many-coloured coarse patches from head to heel." See
page 49, note 19.

[20] Of course Bottom means the make-believe death which is to form the catastrophe
of "our play."

SCENE II.

Athens. A Room in QUINCE'*s House.*

[*Enter* QUINCE, FLUTE, SNOUT, *and* STARVELING.]

QUINCE. Have you sent to Bottom's house? is he come home yet?
STARVELING. He cannot be heard of. Out of doubt, he is transported.[21]
FLUTE. If he come not, then the play is marred; it goes not forward, doth it?
QUINCE. It is not possible: you have not a man in all Athens able to discharge Pyramus but he.
FLUTE. No; he hath simply the best wit of any handicraft man in Athens.
QUINCE. Yea, and the best person too: and he is a very paramour for a sweet voice.
FLUTE. You must say paragon: a paramour is, God bless us, a thing of naught.
[*Enter* SNUG.]
SNUG. Masters, the duke is coming from the temple; and there is two or three lords and ladies more married: if our sport had gone forward, we had all been made men.[22]
FLUTE. O sweet bully Bottom! Thus hath he lost sixpence a day during his life; he could not have 'scaped sixpence a-day; an the duke had not given him sixpence a-day for playing Pyramus, I'll be hanged; he would have deserved it: sixpence a-day in Pyramus, or nothing.

[*Enter* BOTTOM.]

BOTTOM. Where are these lads? where are these hearts?
QUINCE. Bottom!—O most courageous day! O most happy hour!
BOTTOM. Masters, I am to discourse wonders: but ask me not what; for if I tell you, I am not true Athenian. I will tell you everything, right as it fell out.
QUINCE. Let us hear, sweet Bottom.
BOTTOM. Not a word of me. All that I will tell you is, that the duke hath dined. Get your apparel together; good strings to your beards,

---

[21] Starveling's *transported* means the same as Snout's *translated*, used before; that is, *transformed* or *metamorphosed.*

[22] To *make a man* is an old phrase for making a man *rich* or *setting him up;* making his *fortune.*

new ribbons to your pumps; meet presently at the palace; every man look over his part; for the short and the long is, our play is preferred.[23] In any case, let Thisbe have clean linen; and let not him that plays the lion pare his nails, for they shall hang out for the lion's claws. And, most dear actors, eat no onions nor garlic, for we are to utter sweet breath; and I do not doubt but to hear them say it is a sweet comedy. No more words: away! go; away! [*Exeunt.*]

---

[23] *Preferred* is here used in a way somewhat peculiar, meaning, not that the play is chosen in preference to others, but that it is put forward to a chance of favour; that is, *recommended.*

ACT V.

SCENE I.

Athens. An Apartment in the Palace of THESEUS.

[*Enter* THESEUS, HIPPOLYTA, PHILOSTRATE, LORDS, *and* ATTENDANTS.]

HIPPOLYTA. 'Tis strange, my Theseus, that these lovers speak of.
THESEUS. More strange than true. I never may believe
These antique fables, nor these fairy toys.
Lovers and madmen have such seething brains,[1]
Such shaping fantasies, that apprehend
More than cool reason ever comprehends.
The lunatic, the lover, and the poet
Are of imagination all compact:[2]
One sees more devils than vast hell can hold;
That is the madman: the lover, all as frantic,
Sees Helen's beauty in a brow of Egypt:
The poet's eye, in a fine frenzy rolling,
Doth glance from heaven to earth, from earth to heaven;
And as imagination bodies forth
The forms of things unknown, the poet's pen
Turns them to shapes, and gives to airy nothing
A local habitation and a name.
Such tricks hath strong imagination,
That, if it would but apprehend some joy,
It comprehends some bringer of that joy;
Or in the night, imagining some fear,[3]
How easy is a bush supposed a bear?
HIPPOLYTA. But all the story of the night told over,
And all their minds transfigur'd so together,
More witnesseth than fancy's images,
And grows to something of great constancy;[4]

---

[1] To *seethe* is to *boil*; and the notion of the brains boiling in such cases was very common. So in *The Tempest*, v. 1: "The brains, now useless, *boil'd* within the skull." And in *The* Winter's *Tale*, iii. 3: "Would any but these *boil'd* brains of nineteen and two-and-twenty hunt this weather?"

[2] That is, *altogether composed* or *made up* of imagination. Spenser often uses *all* for *altogether*; and Shakespeare has both *all* and *compact* repeatedly in these senses.

[3] *Fear* for *danger*, or the *thing feared*; a frequent usage.

[4] *Constancy* for *consistency* or *congruity*; such as makes a story credible. One of the Latin senses of the word.

But, howsoever, strange and admirable.[5]
THESEUS. Here come the lovers, full of joy and mirth.—

[*Enter* LYSANDER, DEMETRIUS, HERMIA, *and* HELENA.]

Joy, gentle friends! joy and fresh days of love
Accompany your hearts!
LYSANDER. More than to us
Wait in your royal walks, your board, your bed!
THESEUS. Come now; what masques, what dances shall we have,
To wear away this long age of three hours
Between our after-supper and bed-time?
Where is our usual manager of mirth?
What revels are in hand? Is there no play
To ease the anguish of a torturing hour?
Call Philostrate.
PHILOSTRATE. Here, mighty Theseus.
THESEUS. Say, what abridgment[6] have you for this evening?
What masque? what music? How shall we beguile
The lazy time, if not with some delight?
PHILOSTRATE. There is a brief how many sports are ripe;
Make choice of which your highness will see first.

[*Giving a paper.*]

THESEUS [*Reads.*] *The battle with the Centaurs, to be sung*
By an Athenian eunuch to the harp.
We'll none of that: that have I told my love,
In glory of my kinsman Hercules.—
[*Reads.*] *The riot of the tipsy Bacchanals,*
Tearing the Thracian singer in their rage.
That is an old device, and it was play'd
When I from Thebes came last a conqueror.—
[*Reads.*] *The thrice three Muses mourning for the death*
Of learning, late deceased in beggary.
That is some satire, keen and critical,[7]
Not sorting with a nuptial ceremony.—
[*Reads.*] *A tedious brief scene of young Pyramus*

---

[5] *Howsoever* in the old sense of *at all events*; and *admirable* in its proper Latin sense of *wonderful.*

[6] *Abridgment* probably means something that *abridges*, or *shortens*, the time; a *pastime.* Or it may mean a dramatic performance, that crowds the events of a long period into a brief space of time.

[7] *Critical* was sometimes used in the sense of *cynical* or *censorious.* So in Iago's well-known saying, *Othello*, ii. 1: "For I am nothing, if not *critical.*"

And his love Thisbe; very tragical mirth.
Merry and tragical! tedious and brief!
That is hot ice and wondrous strange snow.
How shall we find the concord of this discord?
PHILOSTRATE. A play there is, my lord, some ten words long,
Which is as brief as I have known a play;
But by ten words, my lord, it is too long,
Which makes it tedious: for in all the play
There is not one word apt, one player fitted:
And tragical, my noble lord, it is;
For Pyramus therein doth kill himself:
Which when I saw rehears'd, I must confess,
Made mine eyes water; but more merry tears
The passion of loud laughter never shed.
THESEUS. What are they that do play it?
PHILOSTRATE. Hard-handed men that work in Athens here,
Which never labour'd in their minds till now;
And now have toil'd their unbreathed[8] memories
With this same play against your nuptial.
THESEUS. And we will hear it.
PHILOSTRATE. No, my noble lord,
It is not for you: I have heard it over,
And it is nothing, nothing in the world;
Unless you can find sport in their intents,
Extremely stretch'd and conn'd with cruel pain,
To do you service.
THESEUS. I will hear that play;
For never anything can be amiss
When simpleness and duty tender it.
Go, bring them in: and take your places, ladies.

[*Exit* PHILOSTRATE.]

HIPPOLYTA. I love not to see wretchedness o'er-charged,
And duty in his service perishing.
THESEUS. Why, gentle sweet, you shall see no such thing.
HIPPOLYTA. He says they can do nothing in this kind.
THESEUS. The kinder we, to give them thanks for nothing.
Our sport shall be to take what they mistake:
And what poor duty cannot do,
Noble respect takes it in might, not merit.[9]

---

[8] *Unbreathed* is *unpractised* or *unexercised.* The Poet has to *breathe* repeatedly in the opposite sense. So in *Timon of Athens,* i. 1: "A man *breathed,* as it were, to an untirable and continuate goodness."

Where I have come, great clerks have purposed
To greet me with premeditated welcomes;
Where I have seen them shiver and look pale,
Make periods in the midst of sentences,
Throttle their practis'd accent in their fears,
And, in conclusion, dumbly have broke off,
Not paying me a welcome. Trust me, sweet,
Out of this silence yet I pick'd a welcome;
And in the modesty of fearful duty
I read as much as from the rattling tongue
Of saucy and audacious eloquence.
Love, therefore, and tongue-tied simplicity
In least speak most to my capacity.

[*Re-enter* PHILOSTRATE.]

PHILOSTRATE. So please your grace, the prologue is address'd.[10]
THESEUS. Let him approach. [*Flourish of trumpets.*]

[*Enter the* PROLOGUE.]

PROLOGUE. *If we offend, it is with our good will.*
That you should think, we come not to offend,
But with good will. To show our simple skill,
That is the true beginning of our end.
Consider then, we come but in despite.
We do not come, as minding to content you,
Our true intent is. All for your delight
We are not here. That you should here repent you,
The actors are at hand: and, by their show,
You shall know all that you are like to know.[11] [*Exit.*]

---

[9] According to the ability of the doer, not according to the worth of the thing done. Here, as often, *respect* is *consideration* or *regard.—Clerks*, in the next line, is *learned men*, or *scholars*; the old meaning of the word.

[10] *Address'd* is *ready, prepared*; a common use of the word. So in *Love's Labours Lost*, ii. 1: "And he and his competitors in oath were all *address'd* to meet you, gentle lady, before I came."

[11] Had "this fellow" stood "upon points," his speech would have read nearly as follows:

> If we offend, it is with our good-will
> That you should think we come not to offend;
> But with good-will to show our simple skill:
> That is the true beginning. Of our end
> Consider then: we come; but in despite
> We do not come: as minding to content you,

THESEUS. This fellow doth not stand upon points.
LYSANDER. He hath rid his prologue like a rough colt; he knows not
  the stop. A good moral, my lord: it is not enough to speak, but to
  speak true.
HIPPOLYTA. Indeed he hath played on this prologue like a child on a
  recorder;[12] a sound, but not in government.
THESEUS. His speech was like a tangled chain; nothing impaired, but
  all disordered. Who is next?

[*Enter the* PRESENTER, *with* PYRAMUS *and* THISBE, WALL,
  MOONSHINE, *and* LION, *as in dumb show.*]

PRESENTER. *Gentles, perchance you wonder at this show;*
  But wonder on, till truth make all things plain.
  This man is Pyramus, if you would know;
  This beauteous lady Thisbe is certain.
  This man, with lime and rough-cast, doth present
  Wall, that vile Wall which did these lovers sunder;
  And through Wall's chink, poor souls, they are content
  To whisper, at the which let no man wonder.
  This man, with lanthorn, dog, and bush of thorn,
  Presenteth Moonshine: for, if you will know,
  By moonshine did these lovers think no scorn
  To meet at Ninus' tomb, there, there to woo.
  This grisly beast, which by name Lion hight[13] *by name,*
  The trusty Thisbe, coming first by night,
  Did scare away, or rather did affright;
  And as she fled, her mantle she did fall;
  Which Lion vile with bloody mouth did stain:
  Anon comes Pyramus, sweet youth, and tall,
  And finds his trusty Thisbe's mantle slain;
  Whereat with blade, with bloody blameful blade,
  He bravely broach'd his boiling bloody breast;
  And Thisbe, tarrying in mulberry shade,
  His dagger drew, and died. For all the rest,

Our true intent is all for your delight.
We are not here, that you should here repent you.
The actors are at hand; and, by their show,
You shall know all that you are like to know.

[12] *Recorder* was the name of a soft-toned instrument, something like the flute. So in
Paradise Lost, i. 550: "Anon they move in perfect phalanx to the Dorian mood of flutes
and soft *recorders.*"
[13] *Hight* is an old word for *is called.* So in *Love's Labours Lost,* i. 1: "This child of
fancy, that Armado *hight,* for interim to our studies, shall relate," &c.

Let Lion, Moonshine, Wall, and lovers twain,
At large discourse while here they do remain.

[*Exeunt* PRESENTER, PYRAMUS, THISBE, LION, *and*
MOONSHINE.]

THESEUS. I wonder if the lion be to speak.
DEMETRIUS. No wonder, my lord: one lion may, when many asses
do.
WALL. *In this same interlude it doth befall*
That I, one Snout by name, present a wall:
And such a wall as I would have you think
That had in it a crannied hole or chink,
Through which the lovers, Pyramus and Thisbe,
Did whisper often very secretly.
This loam, this rough-cast, and this stone, doth show
That I am that same wall; the truth is so:
And this the cranny is, right and sinister,
Through which the fearful lovers are to whisper.
THESEUS. Would you desire lime and hair to speak better?
DEMETRIUS. It is the wittiest partition that ever I heard discourse,[14]
my lord.
THESEUS. Pyramus draws near the wall; silence.

[*Enter* PYRAMUS.]

PYRAMUS. *O grim-look'd night! O night with hue so black!*
O night, which ever art when day is not!
O night, O night, alack, alack, alack,
I fear my Thisbe's promise is forgot!—
And thou, O wall, O sweet, O lovely wall,
That stand'st between her father's ground and mine;
Thou wall, O wall, O sweet and lovely wall,
Show me thy chink, to blink through with mine eyne.

[WALL *holds up his fingers.*]

Thanks, courteous wall: Jove shield thee well for this!
But what see what see I? No Thisbe do I see.
O wicked wall, through whom I see no bliss,
Curs'd be thy stones for thus deceiving me!
THESEUS. The wall, methinks, being sensible, should curse again.

_____

[14] An equivoque or pun was no doubt intended here; one sense of *partition* being
that of *dividing* a theme of discourse into heads or topics.

PYRAMUS. No, in truth, sir, he should not. *Deceiving me* is Thisbe's
cue: she is to enter now, and I am to spy her through the wall. You
shall see it will fall pat as I told you.—Yonder she comes.

[*Enter* THISBE.]

THISBE. *O wall, full often hast thou heard my moans,*
For parting my fair Pyramus and me:
My cherry lips have often kiss'd thy stones:
Thy stones with lime and hair knit up in thee.
PYRAMUS. *I see a voice; now will I to the chink,*
To spy an I can hear my Thisbe's face.
Thisbe!
THISBE. *My love! thou art my love, I think.*
PYRAMUS. *Think what thou wilt, I am thy lover's grace;*
And like Limander,[15] *am I trusty still.*
THISBE. *And I like Helen, till the fates me kill.*
PYRAMUS. *Not Shafalus to Procrus was so true.*
THISBE. *As Shafalus to Procrus, I to you.*
PYRAMUS. *O, kiss me through the hole of this vile wall.*
THISBE. *I kiss the wall's hole, not your lips at all.*
PYRAMUS. *Wilt thou at Ninny's tomb meet me straightway?*
THISBE. *'Tide life, 'tide death, I come without delay.*

[*Exeunt* PYRAMUS *and* THISBE.]

WALL. *Thus have I, wall, my part discharged so;*
And, being done, thus Wall away doth go. [*Exit.*]
THESEUS. Now is the mural down between the two neighbours.
DEMETRIUS. No remedy, my lord, when walls are so wilful to hear
without warning.[16]
HIPPOLYTA. This is the silliest stuff that ever I heard.
THESEUS. The best in this kind are but shadows; and the worst are no
worse, if imagination amend them.
HIPPOLYTA. It must be your imagination then, and not theirs.
THESEUS. If we imagine no worse of them than they of themselves,
they may pass for excellent men. Here come two noble beasts in, a
moon and a lion.

---

[15] *Limander* and *Helen*, blunderingly, for *Leander* and *Hero*; as, a little after,
Shafalus and *Procrus* for *Cephalus* and *Procris*. Procris, or Procne was the wife of
Cephalus; and when Aurora fell in love with him, and tried to win his heart, he stuck to
his Procne. See page 61, note 55.
[16] Alluding to the old proverb, "Walls have ears"; which probably grew from the
aptness of walls or partitions to transmit sound.

[LION *and* MOONSHINE.]

LION. *You, ladies, you, whose gentle hearts do fear*
The smallest monstrous mouse that creeps on floor,
May now, perchance, both quake and tremble here,
When lion rough in wildest rage doth roar.
Then know that I, one Snug the joiner, am
A lion fell, nor else no lion's dam:
For, if I should as lion come in strife
Into this place, 'twere pity on my life.
THESEUS. A very gentle beast, and of a good conscience.
DEMETRIUS. The very best at a beast, my lord, that e'er I saw.
LYSANDER. This lion is a very fox for his valour.
THESEUS. True; and a goose for his discretion.
DEMETRIUS. Not so, my lord; for his valour cannot carry his
discretion, and the fox carries the goose.
THESEUS. His discretion, I am sure, cannot carry his valour; for the
goose carries not the fox. It is well; leave it to his discretion, and
let us listen to the moon.
MOONSHINE. *This lanthorn doth the horned Moon present;—*
DEMETRIUS. He should have worn the horns on his head.
THESEUS. He is no crescent, and his horns are invisible within the
circumference.
MOONSHINE. *This lanthorn doth the horned moon present;*
Myself the man i' the moon do seem to be.
THESEUS. This is the greatest error of all the rest: the man should be
put into the lantern. How is it else the man i' the moon?
DEMETRIUS. He dares not come there for the candle: for, you see, it
is already in snuff.[17]
HIPPOLYTA. I am aweary of this moon: would he would change!
THESEUS. It appears, by his small light of discretion, that he is in the
wane: but yet, in courtesy, in all reason, we must stay the time.
LYSANDER. Proceed, moon.
STARVELING. All that I have to say, is to tell you that the lantern is
the moon; I, the man i' the moon; this thorn-bush, my thorn-bush;
and this dog, my dog.[18]

---

[17] A quibble between *snuff* as meaning the cinder of a candle and as meaning
sudden anger. Shakespeare has it repeatedly.

[18] The legend of the Man-in-the-Moon is very ancient, and is often alluded to by the
old Poets. Perhaps it took its origin from the rude and faint resemblance to a man's face
which the full Moon presents. At all events, the notion was common in the days of my
boyhood: the man was talked of by everybody, and I often saw him. And it appears that
he was sometimes introduced upon the English stage. Ben Jonson, in his masque entitled
"News from the New World discovered in the Moon," 1620, makes some of the persons

DEMETRIUS. Why, all these should be in the lantern; for all these are in the moon. But silence; here comes Thisbe.

[*Enter* THISBE.]

THISBE. *This is old Ninny's tomb. Where is my love?*
LION. [*Roaring.*] *O*—— [THISBE *runs off.*]
DEMETRIUS. Well roared, lion.
THESEUS. Well run, Thisbe.
HIPPOLYTA. Well shone, moon.—Truly, the moon shines with a good grace. [LION *tears* THISBE's *mantle, and exit.*]
THESEUS. Well moused,[19] lion.
DEMETRIUS. And so comes Pyramus.
LYSANDER. And then the lion vanishes.

[*Enter* PYRAMUS.]

PYRAMUS. *Sweet moon, I thank thee for thy sunny beams;*
I thank thee, moon, for shining now so bright;
For, by thy gracious golden, glittering gleams,
I trust to take of truest Thisbe's sight.

> *But stay;—O spite!—but mark,—poor knight,*
> *What dreadful dole is here!*
> *Eyes, do you see? how can it be?*
> *O dainty duck! O dear!*
> *Thy mantle good, what, stained with blood?*
> *Approach, ye furies fell!*
> *O fates! come, come, cut thread and thrum;*
> *Quail, rush, conclude, and quell!*

---

tell how Poetry, "the mistress of all discovery," has sent one of her servants to the Moon "in search of truth," and he has just returned; whereupon we have the following:

Fact. Where? which is he? I must see his dog at his girdle, and the bush of thorns at his back, ere I believe it.

1 Herald. Do not trouble your faith then; for, if the bush of thorns should prove a goodly grove of oaks, in what case were you and your expectation?

2 Herald. These are stale ensigns of the *stage's* Man in the Moon, delivered down to you by musty antiquity, and are of as doubtful credit as the makers.

[19] To *mouse* is to *tear in pieces,* as a cat tears a mouse. So in *King John,* ii. 1:

> O, now doth Death line his dead chops with steel;
> The swords of soldiers are his teeth, his fangs;
> And now he feasts, *mousing;* the flesh of men.

THESEUS. This passion, and the death of a dear friend, would go near
to make a man look sad.
HIPPOLYTA. Beshrew my heart, but I pity the man.
PYRAMUS. *O wherefore, nature, didst thou lions frame?*
Since lion vile hath here deflower'd my dear;
Which is—no, no—which was the fairest dame
That lived, that loved, that liked, that look'd with cheer.

Come, tears, confound; out, sword, and wound
The pap of Pyramus,—
Ay, that left pap, Where heart doth hop:
Thus die I, thus, thus, thus. [*Stabs himself.*]
Now am I dead, Now am I fled;
My soul is in the sky:
Tongue, lose thy light! Moon, take thy flight!

[*Exit* MOONSHINE.]

Now die, die, die, die, die.

DEMETRIUS. No die, but an ace, for him; for he is but one.
LYSANDER. Less than an ace, man; for he is dead; he is nothing.
THESEUS. With the help of a surgeon he might yet recover and prove
an ass.
HIPPOLYTA. How chance moonshine is gone before Thisbe comes
back and finds her lover?
THESEUS. She will find him by starlight.—Here she comes; and her
passion ends the play.

[*Re-enter* THISBE.]

HIPPOLYTA. Methinks she should not use a long one for such a
Pyramus: I hope she will be brief.
DEMETRIUS. A mote will turn the balance, which Pyramus, which
Thisbe, is the better—he for a man, God warrant us; she for a
woman, God bless us.
LYSANDER. She hath spied him already with those sweet eyes.
DEMETRIUS. And thus she moans, videlicet.—
THISBE. *Asleep, my love? what, dead, my dove?*
O Pyramus, arise,
Speak, speak. Quite dumb? Dead, dead? A tomb
Must cover thy sweet eyes.
These lily lips, This cherry nose,
These yellow cowslip cheeks,
Are gone, are gone: Lovers, make moan!

> *His eyes were green as leeks.*
> *O Sisters Three, come, come to me,*
>   *With hands as pale as milk;*
> *Lay them in gore, since you have shore*
>   *With shears his thread of silk.*
> *Tongue, not a word: come, trusty sword;*
>   *Come, blade, my breast imbrue;* [*Stabs himself.*]
> *And farewell, friends:—Thus Thisbe ends,—*
>   *Adieu, adieu, adieu.* [*Dies.*]

THESEUS. Moonshine and lion are left to bury the dead.
DEMETRIUS. Ay, and wall too.
BOTTOM. No, I assure you; the wall is down that parted their fathers. Will it please you to see the epilogue, or to hear a Bergomask dance[20] between two of our company?
THESEUS. No epilogue, I pray you; for your play needs no excuse. Never excuse; for when the players are all dead there need none to be blamed. Marry, if he that writ it had played Pyramus, and hang'd himself in Thisbe's garter, it would have been a fine tragedy: and so it is, truly; and very notably discharged. But come, your Bergomask; let your epilogue alone.—

[A *dance by two of the* CLOWNS.]

The iron tongue of midnight hath told twelve:—
Lovers, to bed; 'tis almost fairy time.
I fear we shall out-sleep the coming morn,
As much as we this night have overwatch'd.
This palpable-gross play hath well beguil'd
The heavy gait of night.—Sweet friends, to bed.—
A fortnight hold we this solemnity,
In nightly revels and new jollity. [*Exeunt.*]

[*Enter* PUCK, *with a broom.*]

PUCK. Now the hungry lion roars,[21]

---

[20] A rustic dance framed in imitation of the people of *Bergamasco*, (a province in the state of Venice,) who are ridiculed as being more clownish in their manners and dialect than any other people of Italy. The *lingua rustica* of the buffoons, in the old Italian comedies, is an imitation of their jargon.

[21] Upon this passage Coleridge thus remarks in his *Literary Remains*: "Very Anacreon in perfectness, proportion, grace, and spontaneity! So far it is Greek;—but then add, what wealth, what wild ranging, and yet what compression and condensation, of English fancy! In truth, there is nothing in Anacreon more perfect than these lines, or half so rich and imaginative. They form a speckless diamond."

And the wolf behowls the moon;
Whilst the heavy ploughman snores,
All with weary task fordone.
Now the wasted brands do glow,
Whilst the screech-owl, screeching loud,
Puts the wretch that lies in woe
In remembrance of a shroud.
Now it is the time of night
That the graves, all gaping wide,
Every one lets forth its sprite,
In the church-way paths to glide:
And we fairies, that do run
By the triple Hecate's team
From the presence of the sun,
Following darkness like a dream,
Now are frolic; not a mouse
Shall disturb this hallow'd house:
I am sent with broom before,
To sweep the dust behind the door.[22]

[*Enter* OBERON *and* TITANIA, *with their Train.*]

OBERON.   Through the house give glimmering light,
          By[23] the dead and drowsy fire:
          Every elf and fairy sprite
          Hop as light as bird from briar:

---

[22] That is, "To sweep the dust *from* behind the door." Collier informs us that on the title-page of the tract, *Robin Goodfellow, his Mad Pranks and Merry Jests,* Puck is represented in a wood-cut with a broom over his shoulder. The whole fairy nation, for which he served as prime minister, were great sticklers for cleanliness. In the old ballad entitled *The Merry Pranks of Robin Goodfellow,* and generally ascribed to Ben Jonson, we have the following:

> When house or hearth doth sluttish lie,
> I pinch the maidens black and blue;
> The bed-clothes from the bed pull I,
> And lay them naked all to view:
> 'Twixt sleep and wake I do them take,
> And on the key-cold floor them throw:
> If out they cry, then forth I fly,
> And loudly laugh out, ho, ho, ho!

[23] *By* seems here to have the force of *by means of,*—no uncommon use of the word.—Milton was probably thinking of this passage in his *Il Penseroso*:

> Where glowing embers through the room
> Teach light to counterfeit a gloom.

And this ditty, after me,
Sing and dance it trippingly.
TITANIA. First, rehearse your song by rote,
To each word a warbling note;
Hand in hand, with fairy grace,
Will we sing, and bless this place.

[*Song and Dance.*]

OBERON. Now, until the break of day,
Through this house each fairy stray,
To the best bride-bed will we,
Which by us shall blessed be;[24]
And the issue there create
Ever shall be fortunate.
So shall all the couples three
Ever true in loving be;
And the blots of Nature's hand
Shall not in their issue stand:
Never mole, hare-lip, nor scar,
Nor mark prodigious,[25] such as are
Despised in nativity,
Shall upon their children be.—
With this field-dew consecrate,
Every fairy take his gait;[26]
And each several chamber bless,
Through this palace, with sweet peace;
E'er shall it in safety rest,
And the owner of it blest.
Trip away; make no stay:
Meet me all by break of day.

[*Exeunt* OBERON, TITANIA, *and Train.*]

PUCK. If we shadows have offended,
Think but this,—and all is mended,—
That you have but slumber'd here

---

[24] This ceremony was in old times used at all marriages. Douce has given the formula from the Manual for the use of Salisbury. In the French romance of Melusine, the Bishop who marries her to Raymondin blesses the nuptial bed. The ceremony is there represented in a very ancient cut. The good prelate is sprinkling the parties with holy water. Sometimes, during the benediction, the married couple only *sat* on the bed; but they generally received a portion of the consecrated bread and wine.

[25] *Prodigious* in the Latin sense of *unnatural, portentous,* or *ill-fated.*

[26] That is, take his *way, pursue* his *course.*

While these visions did appear.
And this weak and idle theme,
No more yielding but a dream,
Gentles, do not reprehend;
If you pardon, we will mend.
And, as I am an honest Puck,[27]
If we have unearned luck
Now to 'scape the serpent's tongue,[28]
We will make amends ere long;
Else the Puck a liar call:
So, good night unto you all.
Give me your hands,[29] if we be friends,
And Robin shall restore amends. [*Exit.*]

THE END

---

[27] *Puck*, it seems, was a suspicious name, which makes that this merry, mischievous gentleman does well to assert his honesty. As for the name itself, it was no better than *fiend* or *devil*. In *Pierce Ploughman's Vision*, one personage is called *helle Pouke*. And the name thus occurs in Spenser's *Epithalamion*:

> Ne let *the pouke*, nor other evill sprights,
> Ne let mischievous witches with theyr charmes,
> Ne let hobgoblins, names whose sence we see not,
> Fray us with things that be not.

[28] Honest Puck, it seems, has a mortal dread of being *hissed.*

[29] Clap your hands, give us your applause.

Made in the USA
Las Vegas, NV
31 May 2021